WICCA

Book of Spells

WITCHES' PLANNER 2022

*A Wheel of the Year Grimoire
with Moon Phases, Astrology,
Magical Crafts, and Magic Spells
for Wiccans and Witches*

LISA CHAMBERLAIN

Disclaimer

No part of this publication may be reproduced or transmitted in any form or by any means, mechanical or electronic, including photocopying or recording, or by any information storage and retrieval system, or transmitted by email without permission in writing from the publisher.

While all attempts have been made to verify the information provided in this publication, neither the author nor the publisher assumes any responsibility for errors, omissions, or contrary interpretations of the subject matter herein.

This book is for entertainment purposes only. The views expressed are those of the author alone, and should not be taken as expert instruction or commands. The reader is responsible for his or her own actions.

Adherence to all applicable laws and regulations, including international, federal, state, and local governing professional licensing, business practices, advertising, and all other aspects of doing business in the US, Canada, or any other jurisdiction is the sole responsibility of the purchaser or reader.

Neither the author nor the publisher assumes any responsibility or liability whatsoever on the behalf of the purchaser or reader of these materials.

Any perceived slight of any individual or organization is purely unintentional.

Your Free Gift

Thank you for adding this book to your Wiccan library! To learn more, why not join Lisa's Wiccan community and get an exclusive, free spell book?

The book is a great starting point for anyone looking to try their hand at practicing magic. The ten beginner-friendly spells can help you to create a positive atmosphere within your home, protect yourself from negativity, and attract love, health, and prosperity.

Little Book of Spells is now available to read on your laptop, phone, tablet, Kindle or Nook device!

To download, simply visit the following link:

www.wiccaliving.com/bonus

Get Three Free Audiobooks
from Lisa Chamberlain

Did you know that all of Lisa's books are available in audiobook format? Best of all, you can get **three audiobooks completely free** as part of a 30-day trial with Audible.

Wicca Starter Kit contains three of Lisa's most popular books for beginning Wiccans, all in one convenient place. It's the best and easiest way to learn more about Wicca while also taking audiobooks for a spin! Simply visit:

www.wiccaliving.com/free-wiccan-audiobooks

Alternatively, *Spellbook Starter Kit* is the ideal option for building your magical repertoire using candle and color magic, crystals and mineral stones, and magical herbs. Three spellbooks – over 150 spells – are available in one free volume, here:

www.wiccaliving.com/free-spell-audiobooks

Audible members receive free audiobooks every month, as well as exclusive discounts. It's a great way to experiment and see if audiobook learning works for you.

If you're not satisfied, you can cancel anytime within the trial period. You won't be charged, and you can still keep your books!

Contents

June

July

August

September

October

November

December

Introduction

Welcome to the 2022 Book of Spells Witches' Planner. This is the 2nd annual collaboration of contributors from many walks of Witchery, including Wicca; Traditional, Hedge, and Kitchen Witchcraft; herbalism; divination; shamanism and spirit communication; and various folk magic traditions. These writers have contributed to publications like *The Crooked Path Journal, Witch Way Magazine, Witchology Magazine,* and *Witches and Pagans Magazine,* and published books on many topics relevant to beginning and experienced Witches alike.

The spells, articles, and other gems of information within these pages are meant to help you keep your practice enlivened throughout the year. You'll find some in-depth discussions at the front of the book with a range of ideas for deepening your practice, as well as plenty of Book-of-Shadows-worthy snippets of information on crystals and herbs, magical crafts, rituals, Sabbat celebration ideas, and more—one for each week of the year.

Working with the natural timing of the Universe is a great way to enhance your magical practice, so you'll also find daily information about the phase and location of the Moon, significant astrological events like planetary retrogrades and eclipses, and, of course, the Sabbat days.

When it comes to magical timing, the phase and location of the Moon is often the most important factor. The symbols used in this planner reflect detailed tracking of the lunar cycle, and the Moon's travels through the Zodiac wheel are also noted.

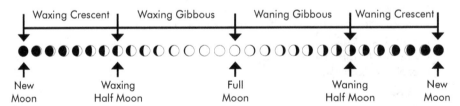

Moon ◯ enters Libra ♎ 4:45 pm

Moon ● v/c 5:39 pm

Generally speaking, the relationship between magic and the Moon can be summed up as follows: as the Moon grows, we work magic for increase; as it wanes, we work magic for decrease. In other words, work with the waxing Moon when you want to bring something into your life, and with the waning Moon when you want to banish or release something from your experience. The Full Moon—the halfway point in the lunar cycle—is a time for appreciating and celebrating our manifestations and achievements, while the New Moon—the beginning of the cycle— is ideal for setting new intentions.

The location of the Moon, or the Zodiac sign it's traveling through at any given moment, can also be significant in terms of magical timing. Different signs are ideal for different magical purposes, which are detailed in the table on pages 10-11. Some Witches find that working when the Moon is void-of-course ("v/c"), or in between one sign and the next, leads to less effective magic, while others experience no difficulty with spells cast at these times. You may want to experiment with this, and see what works best for you.

It's important to note that this planner uses U.S. Eastern Standard Time/ Eastern Daylight Time (depending on which is applicable), so if you live in a different time zone, you'll need to calculate the difference in the hours noted for astrological events. This also means that certain dates may be slightly off, depending on where you live. You can find plenty of time zone converters online to help you make the needed adjustments.

Finally, because the contributors represent such a wide spectrum of magical backgrounds and perspectives on the Craft, you may notice some inconsistencies in the spelling and capitalization of certain terms, as well as a variety of magical terminology. This is to be expected, given the rich diversity of paths within the Witching world, and these differences are celebrated here.

I and the other authors of this book hope you will find it a fun and useful way to integrate magic and Witchcraft into your days in 2022. May you have an incredibly blessed and magical year!

–Lisa Chamberlain

Zodiac Signs and Magical Purposes

Moon in Zodiac sign	Work magic related to...
Aries	new ventures, general health and vitality, self-improvement, difficult conflicts, navigating issues with bureaucracy, leadership, authority, impatience difficult tempers, surgery
Taurus	money, prosperity, real estate, material acquisitions, self-esteem, love, sensuality, gardening and farming, fertility, patience, endurance, commitment, music, the arts, business
Gemini	intelligence, communication, commerce, siblings, writing, teaching, neighbors, dealing with gossip, travel, transportation, public relations, media, networking, adaptability, memory, LGBT issues
Cancer	home, family, mothers, children, traditions, weather and climate, security, integrity, water issues (particularly natural bodies of water), psychic abilities, integrity, listening to and assisting others
Leo	love (platonic), self-confidence, self-expression, performing in public, vacation and leisure time, courage, childbirth, taking risks, good cheer, gambling, amusement, creativity, loyalty, fine arts
Virgo	health and healing, diet, business and trade, tools, employment, intelligence and intellect, co-workers, military and police, exercise and fitness, work ethic, debt, cleansing and purification, hunting, pets

Moon in Zodiac sign	Work magic related to...
Libra	legal matters, justice, marriage, peace, balance, diplomacy, beauty, harmony, team-building, contracts, romance and dating, partnership, art and music, socializing, meeting people, overcoming laziness
Scorpio	regeneration, renewal, sex, death, secrets, divination, psychic development, banishing, willpower, purification, hypnotism, emotional honesty, solitude, courage, transformation, mediumship
Sagittarius	optimism, resilience, generosity, legal matters, education (especially higher education), ethics, dreams, contacting the divine, generosity, fame, publishing, good luck, long journeys, fun, humor, languages
Capricorn	careers, jobs, promotions, fathers, responsibility, solitude, healing from depression, ambition, public recognition, honor, reputation, awards, long term results, government, time management, wisdom,
Aquarius	friendship, acquaintances, politics, electronics, freedom, science, extrasensory development, breaking bad habits, problem solving, objectivity, luck, meeting new people, social justice, hope
Pisces	psychic ability, music, spirituality, criminal matters, widows and orphans, reversing bad luck, finding lost items, charity, self-reflection, past lives, facing fears, endings, water (particularly oceans and salt water), dance, drug and alcohol problems

Sabbats of 2022

Imbolc	February 2 *Imbolc cross-quarter day February 3
Ostara	March 20
Beltane	May 1 *Beltane cross-quarter day May 6
Litha	June 21
Lammas	August 1 *Lammas cross-quarter day August 7
Mabon	September 22
Samhain	October 31 *Samhain cross-quarter day November 7
Yule	December 21

Full Moons of 2022

Wolf Moon	January 17	6:49 pm
Snow Moon	February 16	11:57 am
Storm Moon	March 18	3:18 am
Pink Moon	April 16	2:55 pm
Flower Moon	May 16	12:15 am
Strawberry Moon	June 14	7:51 am
Thunder Moon	July 13	2:38 pm
Corn Moon	August 11	9:36 pm
Harvest Moon	September 10	5:59 am
Hunter's Moon	October 9	4:55 pm
Frost Moon	November 8	6:03 am
Long Nights Moon	December 7	11:09 pm

Eclipses of 2022

Date	Eclipse Type	Time	Zodiac Sign & Degree
April 30	**Partial Solar Eclipse**	4:27 pm	10° Taurus ♉ 28'
May 16	**Total Lunar Eclipse**	12:13 am	25° Scorpio ♏ 18'
October 25	**Partial Solar Eclipse**	6:48 am	2° Scorpio ♏ 00'
November 8	**Total Lunar Eclipse**	6:01 am	16° Taurus ♉ 01'

Planetary Retrogrades of 2022

Planet	Date and Time Retrograde	Date and Time Direct
Uranus ♅	August 19 (2021), 9:40 pm	January 18, 10:26 am
Venus ♀	December 19 (2021), 5:36 am	January 29, 3:46 am
Mercury ☿	January 14, 6:41 am	February 3, 11:13 pm
Pluto ♇	April 29, 2:36 pm	October 8, 5:56 pm
Mercury ☿	May 10, 7:47 am	June 3, 4:00 am
Saturn ♄	June 4, 5:47 pm	October 23, 12:07 am
Neptune ♆	June 28, 3:55 am	December 3, 7:15 pm
Jupiter ♃	July 28, 4:38 pm	November 23, 6:02 pm
Uranus ♅	August 24, 9:54 am	January 22 (2023), 5:58 pm
Mercury ☿	September 9, 11:38 pm	October 2, 5:07 am
Mars ♂	October 30, 9:26 am	January 12 (2023), 3:56 pm
Mercury ☿	December 29, 4:32 am	January 18 (2023), 8:12 am

The Moon, the Witch, and the Stars: Esbats and Astro-Magic

It's often said that no two sunsets are exactly alike. The same can be said of the Full Moon. While this phase of the lunar cycle does have consistent characteristics, such as increased energy and enhanced psychic perception, each instance of a Full Moon has its own distinct energies. These are related to the particular season and month it falls in, as well as any significant astrological phenomena occurring at the time.

Often, esbat celebrations focus on seasonal influences during a Full Moon, and may work with corresponding aspects of the Goddess. Summer esbats, for example, are often devoted to Mother goddesses like Demeter and Brighid, while Winter esbats focus on Crone goddesses such as Hecate and Kali. Traditional names for a Full Moon may also lend shape to the ritual.

There are several names for each Moon, which are borrowed from various Native American traditions, as well as the ancient Celts and, more rarely, Chinese traditions. For example, the Full Moon in January is known variously as the Ice Moon, the Wolf Moon, or the Stay Home Moon. A January esbat ritual might center around the benefits of solitude, strength, or stillness, among other themes.

Alternatively, Witches may focus on the Zodiac sign the Moon is currently traveling through. For example, the Full Moon that occurs between April 20 and May 20 is called the Scorpio Full Moon, which this year falls on May 16. This is a time to reflect on the nature of illusion and to engage in piercing through illusions that are blocking our progress in some way. Magic at this time may be worked for protection from negativity, enhanced intuition, or deeper connection with one's inner power.

Interestingly, the Full Moon is always in the Zodiac sign directly opposite from the Sun, which which poses a bit of a quandary when it comes to goddess alignments. Scorpio is generally associated with Crone aspect, while the seasonally appropriate aspect for Taurus (Spring) would be a Maiden goddess. But you don't have to choose one or the other of these two frameworks in designing an esbat ritual. The beauty of eclectic practice is that you can create your own way of weaving both seasonal and astrological influences together in your ritual and magic, for a balanced approach to tuning into the energies of this powerful phase in the cycle.

Lunar Magic and the Zodiac

Astrological considerations don't only apply to esbats and the Full Moon, however. The Moon spends approximately two and a half days in each Zodiac sign as it spins around the Earth, and each sign contributes its own energies to the cosmic mix—particularly when it comes to humans and emotions. Those who are attuned to these subtle shifts will notice certain patterns in circumstances and behavior that correspond to each sign. For example, when the Moon is in Aries, which is ruled by Mars, people tend to feel more assertive and even argumentative. Events may unfold rapidly at this time, and then come to an equally quick end.

These astrological influences can be used to guide your magical work as well. In the case of Aries, which is located at the beginning of the Zodiac, spells involving beginnings are favored. The Moon in Capricorn is a good time to work for career upgrades, while the Virgo Moon enhances spellwork for health and healing.

Another factor to keep in mind is the "void of course" Moon. When the Moon is en route from one sign to the next, there is a brief period where it isn't in a sign at all. Many Wiccans and other Witches recommend abstaining from spellwork at this time, as the lunar energies are "on break," so to speak, and magic is likely to have little effect. These "void" periods are just a few hours long on average, but occasionally last for a day or more.

Finally, Witches who are really into astrology might also take into account the Moon's position in relation to the planets, particularly when an alignment with one or more planets has a significant energetic effect on events, emotions, and other circumstances. For example, the Moon trine Venus is a good time for spellwork related to meeting new people and improving existing friendships. This energy is enhanced if the Moon is in Aquarius, and especially during the waxing phase.

However, this is more advanced knowledge than most people find necessary, at least when it comes to ritual and magic. Too much detail can definitely end up distracting from your focus at the altar, so if planetary aspects cause more confusion than inspiration, don't worry. There's really no need to become an astrology buff in order to work with the Moon's magical energy. But by observing the basic astrological influences of the Moon's sign, you can enhance your spellwork, and turn each esbat into a unique occasion.

—Lisa Chamberlain

Tarot Journaling

Learning tarot takes dedicated practice, reflection, and studying. There are many methods for becoming familiarized with the cards' meanings, but one effective practice for building a strong connection to tarot is working with a tarot journal. Journaling is a fantastic method for tracking cards you are drawing, how you interpret them, and how your relationship with tarot evolves over time. Most importantly, a tarot journal is a powerful recording that you can use to reflect on how readings manifested in your life. Here are some suggested methods for setting up a dedicated tarot journal, as well as ideas to make it a productive tracker of your work with the cards.

Choosing your tarot journal

First, you'll want to consider whether you'd prefer an electronic journal or a paper journal. The benefit of an electronic journal is that your words can be moved around and organized any way you like. You'll never run out of space in an electronic journal. You can even consider keeping your journal on an online blog, or using a social media platform like Instagram to record pictures along with your entries. On the other hand, one benefit of a paper journal is that it's tangible, something that you can touch and place alongside your tarot cards. A physical journal can allow for time to devote to writing, away from your electronic devices. You can find a blank journal, but there are also tarot journals with templates specific for tarot readings, if you'd like something that is ready to work with when you open it. One fun example is the easy-to-fill-in Daily Tarot Journal, by Tidy Tarot. I personally use a three-ring binder for my tarot journal as a way to easily organize notes into different sections.

What are you going to write about?

At the outset, it's helpful to consider what your purpose is for developing and keeping a tarot journal. You may want to ask yourself what your current goals are in relation to tarot. Are you just starting out and exploring the cards' basic interpretations? Or, are you a seasoned reader who is hoping to take deeper dives into tarot symbolism and history? Do you want to read for other people, or are tarot readings a personal activity for reflection and support? Which deck are you currently using, and how might this influence your journal? As you progress, you may find that your journal contains more than just notes on cards you've pulled in readings—it may also contain favorite tarot spreads, images of tarot cards, drawings, and/or notes from tarot classes.

Below we will look at several ways to capture tarot information in your journal on a regular basis. Keep in mind that they are merely suggestions. Feel free to experiment, and approach your tarot journal in the way that works best for you.

One Card Morning Reading

Many people like to pull one card in the morning as a way to have a message for their day. If you pull one card in the morning, consider journaling about the following questions.

- What are your initial reactions to the card? Do you have any psychic impressions when you look at the card?
- Without looking up meanings, what are your initial interpretations and meanings for this card?
- Are there any symbols that stand out in the card? If so, what are they and what do they mean to you?
- What does your favorite tarot guidebook say this card means?
- If you were interpreting this card for a friend, what messages and information would you share about the upcoming day?

Three Card Reading

A simple three card reading is a popular and enjoyable way of reading that can easily be captured in a tarot journal. You will commonly find that people draw the first card to represent past events, the second card to represent current events, and the third card to represent future events. Three card readings can go beyond this, however. Consider using three card readings to explore the following topics:

- 1. Love 2. Health 3. Money
- 1. Mind 2. Body 3. Spirit
- 1. Yourself 2. Your partner 3. The relationship
- 1. Your goal 2. A plan 3. The outcome
- 1. Challenge 2. Blessing 3. Lesson

Tarot Through the Wheel of the Year

There are many other ways to journal with tarot on a regular basis. One way is to use special tarot spreads that focus on the eight Sabbats of the Wheel of the Year. For an easy start, here are three cards to draw at each holiday, in honor of the holiday's themes and magical significance:

- **Samhain:** 1. Something changing in your life 2. Something to banish in your life 3. Events in the year ahead
- **Yule:** 1. Blessings in your life 2. Where you need healing 3. Where you are being "reborn"
- **Imbolc:** 1. What needs purifying 2. Where to focus creatively 3. What's awakening in your life
- **Ostara:** 1. Where you need balance 2. What is waking up in your life 3. What to grow in your life
- **Beltane:** 1. How love appears in your life 2. How to bring prosperity into your life 3. How you connect with nature and the Fae

- **Litha:** 1. How you are strong 2. How to realize your dreams 3. Your magical talents
- **Lughnasadh:** 1. What needs sacrificing in your life 2. Where you need to remain focused 3. Where there is abundance in your life
- **Mabon:** 1. How to be of service to others 2. Something to be grateful for 3. Transitions in your life

Reflecting on Your Tarot Journal

There is a lot of satisfaction and pride in reviewing the interpretations, research, and expressive entries you create in your journal. Enjoy this practice as much as doing the readings, as it shows how your skills and your relationship with tarot mature over time.

—Kiki Dombrowski

Witchcraft: Social Media Aesthetics vs Real Practice

The path of witchcraft is a beautiful, powerful, and joyful path to be on, especially for beginners. Nothing quite compares with those early days of discovering all the wonders of witchcraft, when you first realize the magic of being a witch, and head out with all the eagerness in the world to get supplies to build your altar and begin practicing. There is so much to learn and so many different areas to explore! Yet unfortunately, those early days can also be tinged with something a little bit dark—the dreaded "social media witchcraft practice."

Social media and the internet in general have become such a big part of our lives and as modern practitioners, this is both a blessing and a curse. This technology blesses us with the ability to connect with likeminded folks near and far, and gives us so many resources at our fingertips to find any information we want very quickly. It provides a place to share ideas, rituals, spells—everything a growing witch could want or need for their practice. There are video platforms, photo platforms, social interaction platforms – pretty much any desire you have, you will find it. I will be the first to admit that I often find myself losing hours online researching different things, and watching a multitude of YouTube videos to get different perspectives on the topic I am researching.

What is the curse, then, you might find yourself asking? For one thing, there is plenty of information out there that is less than ideal and often wholly inaccurate. The underbelly of online witching is that there is as much bad information as there is good, and some of the information being represented as fact is honestly quite terrifyingly atrocious. I once had someone try to convince me that cave people practiced Wicca and they were quite set in their belief that this was fact. I'll admit, that certainly gave me pause because I have never, in my life, heard of such a thing. Ancient peoples practiced their own beautiful sort of spirituality that was current to them at the time and very much region-specific. Misinformation like this leads to the belief that one way is the only way, and that any aspect of a person's practice that doesn't match point for point with another practitioner's personal gnosis or path of spirituality is incorrect.

But a potentially bigger problem is the "witch aesthetic" that has pervaded the mainstream, which can set up unrealistic expectations for beginning witches. Instagram, for example, is filled with gorgeous photos of cottagecore altars, dark academia-looking magical tomes, and purposely decorated spaces to give off a vibe of being "witchy" all of the time. I have seen so many new to the path become intimidated and disheartened because they feel as though they can't live up to the idea of what being a witch is and will often move away from it before they have truly begun studying. The world is such an artistic place with so many amazing and varied visions of what practice is and what it can be, and no one should feel pressured to be like anyone else in the way they design their practice.

Personally my practice is very simple. This comes from my path of being a hedge witch and folk magic practitioner. I keep a very clean altar; everything has its place and it is mostly kept tidy. To look at it, in the context of "likes" on social media, my space would probably come across as very boring. For me, having an overly cluttered altar with all sort of magical accoutrements would drive me nuts. I don't like having herbs, crystals, candles and statuary haphazardly placed on my altar simply to give it an aesthetic. I like everything to be where I want it, with a big space to do my workings. I don't often share pictures of my altar on social media or write about it, because I feel as though my altar is my own and it has its purpose in my life that doesn't need to be widely advertised or shared. (I do that with my garden instead—I'm an oversharer when it comes to my plant babies. But this is what I love to do—take photos of plants and share them with the world, or at least the small corner of the world that pays attention to my social media!)

When it comes to creating your sacred space, there is nothing wrong with a simple set up. A basic altar is still an altar, just as a novelty tarot deck is still a tarot deck. That cute cup you saw in a thrift store that inspired happy feelings? It will be fine as a chalice; the Gods won't be offended if you don't get that gothic-looking goblet that you'll probably never use out of fear of damaging it. Your Book of Shadows can be a simple spiral bound notebook or 3-ring binder, so if you're not confident using a big leather-bound parchment tome, then don't. Most witches will tell you their first magical book was a 3-ring binder or a spiral notebook. We're practical souls at the heart of it, and as you grow your path will grow. You will find yourself wanting to add things to your Book of Shadows and even remove things, and folders are flexible like that.

Social media is a very different world from the actual world, and I would encourage you as a practitioner to find your place in it in a way that suits you. You can, of course, completely abstain from sharing your practice online. There is no one right way to do things—ultimately you need to do what works for you in the best possible way for your circumstances and practice. There are some really wonderful resources out there that will help you grow and adapt on your journey, so brave the wide world and see what you can find. But at the same time, always be mindful of what type of information you consume and what you let come into your sacred space.

—Stacey Carroll

Navigating Retrograding Planets

You don't have to be a Cosmic Witch to work with the unpredictable energy of a retrograding planet. As witches, we often work with the Moon, but the retrograde of the planets provides an excellent opportunity to harness planetary energy in our spell work. All types of Witches can benefit from these planetary movements.

While the most well-known retrograde is Mercury, the other planets in our solar system also cycle through their own retrograde, represented in astrological data with the symbol * Retrograde symbol here or the abbreviation "Rx".

What is a Retrograde?

When a planet moves into its retrograde phase, it appears to go backward in its orbit when viewed from Earth, but it isn't actually moving backward. All the planets move in one direction around the Sun and complete their own cycles. In essence, a retrograde is an illusion. Nonetheless, something about the planet's movement at this time results in certain energies that are felt to varying degrees here on Earth.

When a retrograde occurs, we often feel that things are "off." This planetary movement can feel out of control at times. It's important to learn to work with it instead of fighting against it. Doing so makes it possible to turn the energy around and make the retrograde work in your favor.

The only astrological planets that don't retrograde are the Sun and Moon, since the Earth orbits the Sun, and the Moon orbits the Earth. The outer planets of Jupiter, Saturn, Uranus, Neptune, and Pluto have much longer orbits than the inner planets of Mercury, Venus, and Mars. As a result, the outer planets' retrogrades last longer, but they typically have less of an impact on us than the retrogrades of the inner planets, due to their slower movement.

Planetary cycles around the Sun:

- **Mercury:** *88 days*
- **Venus:** *225 days*
- **Earth:** *365 days*
- **Mars:** *687 days*
- **Jupiter:** *4,333 days*
- **Saturn:** *10,759 days*
- **Uranus:** *30,687 days*
- **Neptune:** *60,190 days*
- **Pluto:** *90,520 days*

As mentioned, the most commonly known retrograde is Mercury, the planet of communication, transportation, travel, and technology. Mercury goes into retrograde for three weeks, three or four times a year. In 2022, Mercury will move into retrograde four times: in January, May, and September, and at the tail end of December. Mercury retrograde is the most-discussed retrograde because it happens so often, and because we often feel its effects the strongest, due to its connection with the mind and technology.

However, the other planets' retrogrades are also important and can still affect us significantly. Each planet has its own energetic properties, and their retrogrades can prominently affect our lives.

The retrograde effect

A retrograde planet is often referred to as a trickster, causing havoc on the areas of our lives governed by planets. For example, while we learned that Mercury governs technology and the mind, it's expected that our technology and forms of communication might experience significant challenges or issues. We may also experience a slowdown of ideas and everything related to clear thinking. When Venus is retrograde, it's usually advised to avoid starting a new relationship or making drastic changes to your appearance, since you may be feeling very differently about these choices once Venus goes direct. Keeping an eye on the relevant areas of your life during each retrograde can help you be on the alert for sudden or unexpected changes, and respond more skillfully.

Planetary Retrograde Keywords

- **Mercury:** *Mind, Communication, Intellect, Reason, Language, Intelligence*
- **Venus:** *Attraction, Love, Relationships, Art, Beauty, Harmony*
- **Mars:** *Aggression, Sex, Action, Desire, Competition, Courage, Passion*
- **Jupiter:** *Luck, Growth, Expansion, Optimism, Abundance, Understanding*
- **Saturn:** *Structure, Law, Restriction, Discipline, Responsibility, Obligation, Ambition*
- **Uranus:** *Eccentricity, Unpredictable Changes, Rebellion, Reformation*
- **Neptune:** *Dreams, Intuition, Mysticism, Imagination, Delusions*
- **Pluto:** *Transformation, Power, Death, Rebirth, Evolution*

Retrogrades and you

It's important to note that not every retrograde that occurs will impact you strongly or even noticeably. There are many times when a retrograde comes and goes, and you may barely feel anything. A way to see how you will feel a retrograde is by noting which sign(s) the planet will be in, and then looking at your natal or birth planets and their sign rulerships. For example, Mercury's first retrograde will occur in Aquarius and Capricorn for the year. Look to your own natal chart. Do you have a Capricorn or Aquarius Sun, Moon, or Ascendant? If so, this may be a stronger retrograde for you than for others who don't have any planets in Capricorn. Using your personal astrology is a great way to see how strongly a retrograde could be felt.

A second way a retrograde may affect you personally in significant ways is if you have inner natal planets that match the planetary rulership. For example, Mercury rules Gemini and Virgo. So, if you have Gemini or Virgo as your Sun, Moon, or Ascendant, expect to feel the turbulent energy of the first retrograde of 2022!

Planetary Rulerships:

- **Mercury:** *Gemini, Virgo*
- **Venus:** *Taurus, Libra*
- **Mars:** *Aries*
- **Jupiter:** *Sagittarius*
- **Saturn:** *Capricorn*
- **Uranus:** *Aquarius*
- **Neptune:** *Pisces*
- **Pluto:** *Scorpio*

Retrogrades in Zodiac signs for 2022

- **Mercury Rx:**
- *In Aquarius and Capricorn (January 14th–February 3rd)*
- *In Gemini and Taurus (May 10th–June 3rd)*
- *In Libra and Virgo (September 9th–October 2nd)*
- *In Capricorn (December 29th–January 18th, 2023)*
- **Venus Rx:** *In Capricorn (December 19th, 2021–January 29th)*
- **Mars Rx:** *In Gemini (October 30th–January 12th, 2023)*
- **Jupiter Rx:** *In Aries and Pisces (July 28th–November 23rd)*
- **Saturn Rx:** *In Aquarius (June 4th–October 23rd)*
- **Uranus Rx:**
- *In Taurus (August 19th, 2021–January 18th)*
- *In Taurus (August 24th–January 22nd, 2023)*
- **Neptune Rx:** *In Pisces (June 28th–December 4th)*
- **Pluto Rx:** *In Capricorn (April 29th–October 8th)*

Most, if not all, planets will turn retrograde at least once each year, and it's helpful to use our own astrological makeup to gauge how they will affect us. But there's no need to be fearful about these planetary movements. After all, it's rare to have long periods of time without at least one planet in retrograde. In other words, retrogrades are a normal part of life. Consider your experiences an opportunity to learn more about astrology and how it relates to your own life, and enjoy the journey.

—Severina Sosa

Creating an Ancestral Altar

Ancestral altars are primarily a way to honor and connect with your ancestors, whether these ancestors be of blood, lineage, or affinity. For some practitioners, an ancestral altar is seasonal, often set up during Samhain and/or Dia de los Muertos to remember those we've lost and invite them to visit us while the veil is thin. Others use ancestral altars to enhance magical workings and manifest abundance in their own lives, as our ancestors generally want what is best for us. Whether we use them seasonally or year-round, creating an ancestral altar is a way for us to acknowledge and honor our ancestors, call upon their guidance and assistance, communicate with passed loved ones, and even heal ancestral wounds.

It should be mentioned now that your ancestral altar should only include those you wish to maintain a relationship with, whether they be blood related, close friends, or even famous people you have a deep connection with. If you have a problematic relative, you are not obligated to pay tribute to them nor continue an abusive relationship. Just because they are blood related, does not mean they are deserving of your energy. I will be the first to say my paternal grandfather is not welcome on my altar at this time, due to the trauma he inflicted on my family. I know this may sound mean, but you are never obligated to maintain relationships with your abusers or those that caused significant family trauma, unless you are open to it. Be sure you are only inviting the ancestors to your altar that you want to have there.

Preparation

Before setting up your altar, you need to designate, cleanse, and consecrate a space for it. Your ancestral altar should be in a prominent location in the home, somewhere your ancestors can feel a part of the family and partake in family routines. Having it somewhere you visit and interact with often also reminds you to pay tribute to your ancestors and maintain good spiritual health with the altar. Placing it somewhere out of the way brings "out of sight, out of mind" into play, making it harder for you to remember to maintain the altar. You should also not place your ancestral altar in your bedroom. This altar will also become a spiritual highway, the energy of which can negatively affect your sleep and dreams. Placing it in your bedroom can also be seen as disrespectful (and honestly, who wants their ancestors watching them in the bedroom? I know I don't).

Once you have found a location and selected a surface, such as a shelf or a small table, you need to cleanse and consecrate the area and the altar itself. There are a number of ways you can do this, including smoke-cleansing with herbs, asperging with consecrated water, or washing with a mixture of water and ammonia, salt water, Florida Water, or rose water. I personally use a combination of methods, using both smoke and salt water for cleansing. To consecrate and bless the altar, wipe it down with Holy water or blessing oils, or say a simple spell prayer dedicating the space to your ancestral altar. I prefer using blessing oils of my own design and reciting a simple poem to consecrate my space and dedicate it to ancestral work.

Next, cover your altar with a cloth of your choice. Some Eastern traditions require the cloth be red, while hoodoo suggests the cloth be made of natural fiber. The Celts encouraged the use of a fringed cloth. Go with the color, texture, and/or tradition that speaks most to you.

Assembly

Each item you place on your altar should hold significance and be used with the intention of inviting your ancestors to the space. Before you begin adding pictures and personal items, however, start with the basics: the Elements. Most ancestral altars include a representation of each element. Candles, especially white seven-day candles, are the most common representation of Fire. White candles help light the way for spirits to find your altar and carry messages to the other side. For Water, a glass or bowl of water is used. It's important to change the water daily, to keep the energy from getting stagnant—this water is an offering to the spirits, as well as a portal through which to speak to them. Incense is used to represent Air, providing a sweet scent as an offering to your ancestors and to carry your intentions to the spirit realm. The Earth representation can take many forms, such as a bowl of salt to protect against unwanted spirits, a loaf of bread, a cigar, flowers, crystals, or even an object sacred to an ancestor featured on the altar. Whatever you choose, be sure each item holds meaning, and replace organic materials (bread, flowers, etc.) often.

Next, begin adding photos, belongings, or the written names of your ancestors to your altar. How you decide to place these items is completely up to you, but it should not be cluttered so that energy can flow freely. Finish your altar with food, libations, tobacco, ancestral money, coins, or flowers as offerings. Like the elemental representations, these should be changed often. Feel free to speak with your ancestors to personalize their offerings. My maternal grandmother likes McDonalds cheeseburgers and fries. Some of your ancestors may ask for items from their homeland. Do your best to honor their wishes.

Once your altar is set up, invite your ancestors to join you there. I encourage you to speak from the heart, instead of writing a fancy invocation.

—*Autumn Willow*

Carnivorous Plants in Magic

Carnivorous plants are looked upon with fascination, but they are rarely discussed, let alone used, in witchcraft. Maybe this is because their carnivorous nature—ingesting bugs for sustenance rather than nutrients from the soil—sounds a bit more like darker magick. Maybe it's because they are less available and so more "unknown" than other plants, or maybe it's because we don't talk about them as much as other plants. No matter the reason, carnivorous plants are essentially forgotten in the green witch's arsenal, but they can offer so much to our witchcraft practices.

There are a variety of carnivorous plants and they work in a variety of ways, but they all evolved into their carnivorous nature because of a need to survive, as their own soil doesn't provide enough nutrients for them to thrive. Over time, they found a way to fill that need, but they do it in various ways; while we're used to the "spring trap" nature of the popular Venus fly trap, other carnivorous plants use different traps to ensnare prey.

Pitchers, for instance, use the pitfall trap, which lures in the bug with the temptation of sweet nectar on the rim of the plant's large oblong "pitcher" bowl. The bug succumbs to the slippery sides of the pitcher and slips down to the bottom of the bowl, where it slowly drowns and is digested by the plant. Other plants use sticky adhesives to trap the bug, and some utilize strong, thin hairs along thin tubes, which don't allow the bug to back its way out of the trap. And depending on the size of the particular carnivorous plant, mice and lizards may meet the same fate.

Much like how these plants nibble away at a "pest," we can use carnivorous plants in our magick as symbols of protection, banishing habits or spiritual pests, and removing toxic people from our spaces as well as our hearts. But carnivorous plants offer another element that other banishing plants don't, and that's resilience and resourcefulness. Not only do these plants remove bothersome pests, but they literally grow from the experience—a way of living they had to design themselves in order to thrive. When we use this symbolism in our banishing and protective work, we can also include the intentions of resilience and strength. Having a plant that incorporates both intentions is, in itself, resourceful.

The "unknown" quality of carnivorous plants also lends them the same status as the poisonous plants we may avoid. Poisonous plants offer banishment and protection because they are toxic, but we often don't use them because they are unsafe. Carnivorous plants are a great substitution for these poisonous plants because they have the same aura of being "feared yet respected," but are not toxic to humans and animals, making them a safer alternative.

Use carnivorous plants much like you would other plants. Crush the dried leaves or heads and burn them in ritual, add them to protective sachets when on the go, or place living or dried plant material in a spell bottle for protection. Or, simply place the living plant in a window sill or by the main threshold of the home to protect it and banish any entities wishing to enter.

For a go-to spell for banishing habits, gather and dry the pitcher portion of the pitcher plant. When dried, add in oak bark for strength, and begonia, which, in the Victorian Language of Flowers, symbolizes the telling or exposing of a secret. Add in nettle for honoring your frustration over the habit and grind the ingredients together. Place this mixture on a lit charcoal disk in a fire-safe dish. As the smoke rolls upward, sit and think about your habit and how it impacts you negatively. Visualize these negative parts rolling, like smoke, into a sphere. It tumbles and undulates with the energy you've given it over time. When you feel you've captured its negative essence, state:

> "The smoke drifts to aether, and so does the habit
> The weak and worn fibers of my overall fabric
> The obsession, temptation, a constant compulsion
> A mind plaque that taps into inner indulgence
> I take to the broom and sweep through the rafters
> The mental attic in which this habit is captured
> Perhaps in a mindset, in memory, it saved me
> But even crows leave their their homestead when the nest gets too shaky."

Blow into the smoke to disturb its pathway and watch the smoke dissipate.

This spell utilizes a bit of sympathetic magick in that as the herbs burn and the smoke drifts from you, so does the habit, and in its place are the courage and strength needed to move beyond it. You may have to repeat the spell, along with daily mindfulness practices, to keep the habit from returning.

—*Sarah Justice*

Snakes, Water, and Celtic Healing Goddesses

What does it mean to have snakes, water, and healing Goddesses together?

The peak of my spiritual initiation was a journey to a Goddess's temple that held numerous pools of water set into the tiled floor. This Goddess challenged me, baptized me, and then told me how I am meant to serve Her. Since then, I've spent quite a bit of time trying to identify Her, based on how Her temple appeared to me, the attributes I glimpsed of Her, and the command She gave me. Regardless of Her name, I have worshipped this Goddess for years, serving Her by doing the work She commanded me to do, as best I can. But it helps to identify Her, as it gives me better knowledge of how She prefers to be worshiped and served. Two Celtic Goddesses of healing waters have remained my best guesses over the years: Sirona and Sulis Minerva.

Sirona was worshiped widely across Roman Gaul. The Romans perceived Her as being similar to their Goddess Hygeia, the daughter of Aesclepius, who himself was a healer and son of Apollo. Like Hygeia, Sirona was depicted with snakes and eggs. The eggs, of course, represent fertility and new life. Snakes have a rich and complex symbology, especially when included within images of healing water Goddesses, which we'll discuss further in a moment.

Sirona was worshiped at mineral springs, often thermal springs, which were also wellness centers for Romans. These springs were frequented because of their curative effects on the body, as well as cleanliness. She was a consort of Apollo in Roman Gaul, who appears with her at times as the syncretized Apollo Grannus. Grannus is a Gaulish God worshiped at a number of hot springs and is associated, like Apollo, with light and warmth as well as healing waters. Apollo Himself was worshiped and prayed in many healing temples that also served as health centers. These temples housed Aesculapian snakes—harmless creatures—that would, it was hoped, confer healing to the patients through their association with this healing God. Patients would sleep overnight at the temples in the hopes of dreaming of their cure, which would be interpreted by priests. This practice, called dream incubation, was practiced at temples in which Sirona was worshiped.

Sulis Minerva was a syncretized Goddess worshiped by both Britons and Romans in Bath, England, where the Romans built a large and elaborate bath complex around the site of a natural mineral hot spring worshiped even earlier by the Britons. Sulis was the Britons' local Goddess of the ancient spring, and Minerva was a Roman Goddess of medicine and wisdom, among other things. The site at Bath included a temple to Sulis Minerva as well as rooms for healing dream incubation.

It also includes a large, stunning gorgoneion—an image of a creature with living snakes for hair. Many of us are familiar with how Minerva received the head of Medusa, one of the Gorgon sisters, and wore it on her breastplate. Intriguingly, the circular gorgoneion at Bath is not feminine, like Medusa, but masculine, with a flowing beard and mustache. His locks of hair resemble rivulets of water flowing from His face as well as snakes. In a sense, He appears like a watery version of a Green Man. While this gorgoneion is unnamed, I have long associated Him with Grannus, mentioned above as the consort of Sirona and Gaulish god syncretized with Apollo.

While not credited with healing, the British goddess Verbeia is also associated with snakes. In icons of Her, She is depicted wearing a long pleated skirt and holding two snakes, one in each hand. The snakes represent flowing water, as She is believed to be the Goddess of the River Wharfe. The fact that snakes are so consistently associated with Her gives us some clue about how to interpret the associations of snakes with Sirona and Sulis. As with Verbeia's iconography, snakes move in similar ways that rivulets of water flow through channels—twisting and writhing along worn paths. And, indeed, there are snakes that occupy waters. I'm thinking of the harmless snakes I often find in and around the water of my beloved creeks near my home.

But the symbolism isn't limited to physical resemblance or proximity between snakes and water. Snakes shed their skins routinely, emerging glossy and fresh from dry husks. Because of this, they have long symbolized healing, regeneration, and eternity for many peoples around the world. Water, too, heals and regenerates us. Water cycles endlessly through weather patterns: evaporation from bodies of water becomes mist and clouds, which grow heavy and condense, then precipitate as rain, flowing into rivers and lakes and the ocean once again. The rain that fell aeons ago is the same rain that falls now. It is eternal.

Snakes also symbolize wisdom, for their habit of holing up in the mysterious earth in winter and emerging again in the spring. The underworld—the inside of the earth itself, where the dead go—is a place of secret knowledge as well as fertility, because it is also the place where seeds are buried, become fertile, and burst forth as nourishing plants.

Clearly, Celtic peoples believed in the powers of healing waters, especially thermal and mineral springs where they worshiped their healing Gods and Goddesses. In these special places, we can wash away the physical and spiritual grime that we accumulate over time. We can be baptized by sacred waters. And we can emerge, like snakes, shining and renewed.

—Heidi Hall

Natural and Witchy Cleaning Products

You don't need to wait until spring to deep-clean your space. Witchy cleaning can connect you to the natural world during any time of the year, with only a few ingredients.

Working with the natural world as a witch often involves more than burning sage for cleansing or feeling the earth beneath your feet during grounding. It also includes incorporating the natural world into your daily life, while honoring the planet. Witches can achieve this by choosing or creating natural alternatives to harmful chemicals, such as those found in a majority of our cleaning products. These chemicals are harmful to what's important: our families and our environment.

Natural cleaning products are better for the environment due to less harmful ingredients, and often come in more eco-friendly packaging. They also tend to be better for more surfaces like counters and other household surfaces.

Choosing natural alternatives can also eliminate harmful skin irritants or respiratory irritants like perfumes, synthetic fragrances, ammonia, chlorine, bleach, dyes, and sulfates. Creating your own natural cleaning products ensures the cleanliness and care for what matters, our family and environment. And the simplest way to ensure that you know what's in your cleaning products is to make them yourself.

Cleaning in general can visually improve your space and help remove unwanted energies and germs. Creating your own magical cleaning mixtures also allows you the ability to alter the surrounding energy of your entire home.

Natural Multi-Purpose Rinse Recipe

The recipe below is a natural multi-purpose rinse that can be adjusted with different herbs, lemon juices, or essential oils. Substitutions can be a great way to practice exploring different ingredients and properties. The recipe calls for vinegar as the main cleaning agent. The acidic nature of vinegar can dissolve dirt, grease, and grime and tackle harmful bacteria.

A natural rinse can be used on floors, appliances, counters, tables, windows, and laminate surfaces. Note that vinegar may dull granite or other stone tiles, so do a patch test first. Some hardwood surface finishings may not agree with the acidity of vinegar, either. If this is the case, replace the vinegar with the manufacturer's recommended ingredients. When in doubt, you can skip the vinegar and add a drop of eco-friendly soap, such as Dr. Bronner's organic soaps.

Strain the mixture before you use a cloth or spray bottle to avoid smaller herbs getting stuck in cloths or nozzles getting blocked. You can also substitute some essential oils for missing herbs. To boost your spray's cleaning powder, you can also add a tsp of baking soda.

If you're pressed for time, you can also warm the mixture in a pot on the stove instead of a bucket, and treat the mixture as a tea-type infusion.

You will need:

- ¼ cup white distilled vinegar
- 1 bucket or bowl
- 2½ cups water
- Sheet of cheesecloth for straining
- 750 ml spray bottle
- Funnel
- Cleaning cloth
- Mint for banishing and protection
- Lavender for consecration, peace, and cleansing
- Basil for calming, abundance, and harmony
- Lemon for renewal and happiness
- Rosemary for protection and purification

Instructions:

1. Gather your materials and begin creating your infusion.
2. Mix equal parts of your herbs into your bucket or bowl and top with vinegar and water.
3. Pass your hand clockwise over the bowl and set your intentions for the mixture.
4. Allow the mixture to infuse for up to fifteen minutes before straining. The longer the better. If you are able, allow to infuse overnight.
5. Strain the mixture into your spray bottle, discarding the spent herbs into your compost.
6. To use, spray into a cloth or on the surface and rub in repetitive motions to allow you time to focus on your intentions.
7. To boost the power of the cleaner, add an incantation such as: "With this spray, I clean and clear away all that is unwanted from this space."
8. Repeat the incantation each time you use the spray. If sealed and stored properly, the mixture can last for up to a year.

The next time that you have to clean your altar area, you'll be able to clean with intention with natural alternatives for peace of mind. Enjoy customizing the scent of your spray and have some fun. If you would like to leave some herbs in your spray, try a lemon rind or a large, dried sprig of any of the herbs listed in the ingredients above.

—Ambrosia Hawthorn

December/January

27 Monday

Moon ◐ in Libra ♎

28 Tuesday

Moon ◐ in Libra ♎
Moon ◐ v/c 4:10 pm
Moon ◐ enters Scorpio ♏ 4:16 pm
Jupiter ♃ enters Pisces ♓ 11:09 pm

29 Wednesday

Moon ◐ in Scorpio ♏

30 Thursday

Moon ◐ in Scorpio ♏
Moon ◐ v/c 12:11 pm
Moon ◐ enters Sagittarius ♐ 6:08 pm

31 Friday

Moon ● in Sagittarius ♐

A Wheel of New Years

For many people, New Year's Day offers a welcome fresh energy, and the promise of new beginnings. But did you know that there are many days throughout the yearly calendar that present the same opportunity? Before the universal adoption of the Gregorian calendar, the start of a new year was typically based on ancient calendars, religious traditions, and lunar and solar cycles, and varied widely from culture to culture.

For example, the Chinese New Year typically falls on the second new moon after the Winter Solstice. The Jewish holiday of Rosh Hashanah (which means "head of the year") begins on the first day of the month of Tishrei, typically in September. The Hindu New Year usually falls in mid March or April, and goes by many names, including Vikram Samvat, Ugadi, and Gudi Padwa.

For Wiccans, the New Year can fall on one of two occasions, depending on the tradition you follow. Yule is recognized as the New Year for many, as it is the time of the rebirth of the Sun God. However, many follow the Celtic Wiccan tradition of Samhain as the New Year.

Your birthday is another type of New Year. Known in astrology as your "solar return," it's the beginning of a new year for you personally, and can be a time to set intentions for your own growth over the coming 12 months. (By the way, the new astrological year begins with the first day of Aries, which coincides with the Spring Equinox.)

So if you're not feeling particularly inspired on January 1st, know that there are plenty of alternative opportunities to explore and celebrate!

—*Lisa Chamberlain*

1 Saturday

Moon ● in Sagittarius ♐
Moon ● v/c 3:16 am
Moon ● enters Capricorn ♑ 6:02 pm

2 Sunday

Mercury ☿ enters Aquarius ♒ 2:09 am
New Moon ● in Capricorn ♑ 1:33 pm

3 Monday

Moon ● in Capricorn ♑
Moon ● v/c 11:21 am
Moon ● enters Aquarius ♒ 5:44 pm

4 Tuesday

Moon ● in Aquarius ♒
Moon ● v/c 7:45 pm

5 Wednesday

Moon ◑ enters Pisces ♓ 7:16 pm

6 Thursday

Moon ◑ in Pisces ♓

7 Friday

Moon ◐ in Pisces ♓
Moon ◐ v/c 5:24 pm

Tea Blessing Ritual

Tea originated as a beverage in ancient China, and has been enjoyed by cultures around the world for centuries. All caffeinated tea stems from different varieties of one plant species: *Camellia sinensis*. Different methods for processing the leaves result in either white, green, yellow, oolong, black or dark teas. Tea drinking is considered a spiritual practice in Buddhism, and can offer many healing properties. Its herbal sister, a tea-less tisane or infusion, offers a way for herbal remedies to reach your system. Both caffeinated and herbal teas can be used in magic. Blessing your tea enchants it and prepares it for use in rituals.

To bless your tea, place your steaming mug in the center of the altar. Light four white candles and place them around the tea to craft a circle of protection and hallow the space. Stir with your finger or spoon: deosil for charging it with positivity and abundance, or widdershins for cleansing of negativity. Add a circle of salt around the cup or pot. State:

> *"A blessed potion, elixir divine,*
> *as nurturing as milk, as rich as wine.*
> *Intentions are set with a hearty sip;*
> *to honor my spirit, who lies within.*
> *to honor the Spirit who rests above;*
> *who glides in the aether like the strong-hearted dove."*

Pick up the cup and envision a flow of energy, from the cup through your left hand, into your body, then through your right hand and into the cup again: a divine circle. Meditate on this flow of energy while you sip your tea, and enjoy the refreshing sense of spiritual focus it brings.

—Sarah Justice

8 Saturday

Moon ☽ enters Aries ♈ 12:26 am

9 Sunday

Moon ☽ in Aries ♈
Waxing Half Moon ☽ 1:12 pm

January

10 Monday

Moon ☽ in Aries ♈
Moon ☽ v/c 2:23 am
Moon ☽ enters Taurus ♉ 9:47 am

11 Tuesday

Moon ☽ in Taurus ♉

12 Wednesday

Moon ☽ in Taurus ♉
Moon ☽ v/c 2:39 pm
Moon ☽ enters Gemini ♊ 10:08 pm

13 Thursday

Moon ☽ in Gemini ♊

14 Friday

Moon ☽ in Gemini ♊
Mercury ☿ ℞ 6:41 am
Moon ☽ v/c 9:22 pm

Mercury retrograde until February 3

Set in Eastern Standard Time (EST)

Lavender Milk Bath

Historically, ritual bathing has been part of many cultures around the world, and is used by folk practitioners as a way to remove negativity, hexes, and even stubborn curses so the person can be born anew. Milk baths are potent purifiers and cleansers, able to remove even the most stubborn of unwanted energies. When you exit a milk bath, all that will remain is you and your own natural energy.

In this milk bath, lavender is used to soothe your aura and focus your mind inward. While you can use this bath before any spell work, it's particularly ideal for spells pertaining to psychic or dream work, astral travel, and moon magic.

You will need:

- ½ cup baking soda
- 1½ cups powdered whole milk, goat's milk, or coconut milk
- 2 tablespoons dried lavender flowers
- 10–15 drops of lavender essential oil

Instructions:

1. Combine all the ingredients into a bowl and mix until well combined. Store in an airtight container, preferably glass, and away from moisture.
2. Draw a hot bath and add half the mixture to the water. Stir counterclockwise to banish unwanted energies. If you want, you can chant your intention while bathing. Bathe for 15-30 minutes, or until you feel purified. By the end, you may notice the bath smells foul. This is an indication that energies have been removed from your person. Rinse off with plain water to flush all the impurities away, and either air dry or use a white towel to pat yourself dry. Do not rub. **—Autumn Willow**

---

15 Saturday

Moon ○ enters Cancer ♋ 11:11 am

---

16 Sunday

Moon ○ in Cancer ♋

January

17 Monday

Full Moon ○ in Cancer ♋ 6:49 pm
Moon ○ v/c 6:49 pm
Moon ○ enters Leo ♌ 11:02 pm

Wolf Moon

18 Tuesday

Moon ○ in Leo ♌
Uranus ♅ D 10:26 am

19 Wednesday

Moon ○ in Leo ♌
Sun ☉ enters Aquarius ♒ 9:38 pm

Sun enters Aquarius (Air)

20 Thursday

Moon ◑ in Leo ♌
Moon ◑ v/c 3:16 am
Moon ◑ enters Virgo ♍ 9:03 am

21 Friday

Moon ◑ in Virgo ♍

40

Moon Phase Tea Mini Ritual

Working with the Moon phases is a great way to tap into their energies, from manifesting new beginnings with the New Moon to celebrating the fulfillment of endeavors with the Full. This tea recipe and mini ritual can be performed at each quarter of the lunar cycle to honor each of the phases and their meanings.

An easy way to learn to flow with the rhythms of the Moon is to remember the following: when the Moon begins to grow after a New Moon, it's waxing, so the energy is growing. After the Moon turns Full, it begins to wane, and so does its energy. Use the First Quarter Moon (or Waxing Half) for harnessing action and the Last Quarter (or Waning Half) for introspection and letting go.

You will need:

- Kettle
- Mug
- 2–3 mint leaves
- 1–2 lavender sprigs
- 1 rosemary sprig
- 3–4 chamomile flowers

Instructions:

1. Cleanse your space and prepare the herbs. You can substitute nettle, rose, hibiscus, calendula, or passionflower for any of the above ingredients.
2. Boil water in a kettle and set your intentions.
3. Add all the herbs to the mug. Remove kettle from the heat.
4. Pour the boiled water over the plant material and say:
    "With these botanicals and herbs I instill,
    My intentions under the moon to fulfill."
5. Meditate on your intentions for ten minutes while your tea brews and cools.
6. Drink the tea while you reflect on the Moon phase and its energy.

—Severina Sosa

22 Saturday

Moon ☽ in Virgo ♍
Moon ☽ v/c 2:46 pm
Moon ☽ enters Libra ♎ 5:03 pm

23 Sunday

Moon ☽ in Libra ♎

January

24 Monday

Moon ☽ in Libra ♎
Mars ♂ enters Capricorn ♑ 7:52 am
Moon ☽ v/c 5:10 pm
Moon ☽ enters Scorpio ♏ 10:56 pm

25 Tuesday

Waning Half Moon ☽ in Scorpio ♏ 8:40 am
Mercury ☿ enters Capricorn ♑ 10:04 pm

26 Wednesday

Moon ☽ in Scorpio ♏

27 Thursday

Moon ☽ in Scorpio ♏
Moon ☽ v/c 12:28 am
Moon ☽ enters Sagittarius ♐ 2:35 am

28 Friday

Moon ☽ in Sagittarius ♐
Moon ☽ v/c 2:00 pm

Set in Eastern Standard Time (EST)

Ritual Dance to Wake the Earth

By the time of late winter, many of us in northern climates have been indoors for months. This ritual offers a means to reconnect spiritually with the energies of Mother Earth and her ever-shifting seasons. If you don't know how to safely build an outdoor fire, be sure to learn how before attempting this working.

You will need:

- Supplies to make a fire (kindling and logs, a fire pit or bowl, a lighter and fire starter, etc.)
- Strong, warm boots and clothing that is warm but unrestrictive

Instructions:

1. At the end of winter, when the weather is still cool but the frost is melting, go out and build a fire. When the fire is hot and large enough, stomp your feet slowly in a circle around the fire. Find your rhythm: *thump, thump, thump.* Experiment with different rhythms in your footsteps, shuffling and stomping and tapping your feet. Follow your intuition; don't worry about making mistakes. Feel it out and trust yourself: trust the music in you.
2. As you stamp out the beat, envision that your feet are knocking on the doors of the earth, waking all the sleeping spirits within. You are waking them from their dormancy, urging them to stretch themselves and push upward toward the surface, toward the air and the light. You are also pressing your living energy into the earth, warming it, causing the spirits of cold that have threaded their fingers over the soil to flee.
3. When the fire goes out, or you are tired, stop and say aloud, *"Winter is gone. Spring is come."* Pour water over the fire, clean up, and walk away softly.

—Heidi Hall

29 Saturday

Venus ♀ D 3:46 am
Moon ☽ enters Capricorn ♑ 4:09 am

30 Sunday

Moon ☽ in Capricorn ♑
Moon ☽ v/c 11:43 pm

31 Monday

Moon ● enters Aquarius ≈ 4:42 am

---

1 Tuesday

New Moon ● in Aquarius ≈ 12:45 am
Moon ● v/c 6:01 am

---

2 Wednesday

Moon ● enters Pisces ♓ 6:00 am

Imbolc

---

3 Thursday

Moon ● in Pisces ♓
Mercury ☿ D 11:13 pm

Imbolc cross-quarter day 3:57 pm

Mercury direct

---

4 Friday

Moon ● in Pisces ♓
Moon ● v/c 4:41 am
Moon ● enters Aries ♈ 9:57 am

Imbolc Herbal Healing & Nourishing Balm

Imbolc marks the first stirrings of Spring, the returning light of the Sun, and the fertility of the earth. As the days grow longer and begin to warm, new life sprouts all around us. It's a time to rejoice in the Sun's healing energy.

One way to harness the magical energy available at this time is through nourishing and healing ourselves. Our skin often takes a beating during the winter months, and it could use a refreshing balm to help it renew and thrive. This balm soothes dry skin and can be adapted to your scent preferences.

You will need:

- ¼ cup white beeswax pastilles
- ⅓ cup virgin coconut oil
- Medium microwave-safe bowl
- ⅓ cup carrier oil such as almond, olive, or jojoba
- ½ tbsp vitamin E oil
- 9 oz worth of small tins or jars

Instructions:

1. Gather your materials and cleanse your sacred space.
2. Microwave the beeswax and coconut oil in a microwave-safe bowl for 30-second increments until the mixture is mostly melted.
3. Stir the remaining beeswax until thoroughly combined. Do not allow it to boil.
4. Remove from the microwave and stir in the carrier and vitamin E oils.
5. Focus on your intentions to heal and nourish and say:

> *"With this balm, I heal Winter's chill,*
> *With this balm, I nourish Spring's will."*

6. Pour the balm into your tins or jars and allow it to be fully set.
7. When ready, apply to your skin and repeat the incantation with each use.

—Ambrosia Hawthorn

---

5 Saturday

Moon ☽ in Aries ♈

---

6 Sunday

Moon ☽ in Aries ♈
Moon ☽ v/c 12:21 pm
Moon ☽ enters Taurus ♉ 5:53 pm

February

7 Monday

Moon ☽ in Taurus ♉

8 Tuesday

Waxing Half Moon ☽ in Taurus ♉ 8:50 am
Moon ☽ v/c 11:48 pm

9 Wednesday

Moon ☽ enters Gemini ♊ 5:27 am

10 Thursday

Moon ☽ in Gemini ♊

11 Friday

Moon ☽ in Gemini ♊
Moon ☽ v/c 3:23 am
Moon ☽ enters Cancer ♋ 6:27 pm

Set in Eastern Standard Time (EST)

Book of Shadows or Grimoire?

When you begin your magical practice, you may decide to create a Book of Shadows that holds your spells, rituals, and other information that will grow with you as you develop along your path. For many beginners, this may bring to mind the giant family grimoire from Practical Magic, with its enchanting illustrations and secret spells. But what is the difference between a Book of Shadows and a grimoire?

A grimoire is a book of research, of spells and rituals, summoning, spirit information and more. There are whole spiritual practices built upon the grimoires of medieval times. Some famous ones are The Keys of Solomon, the Book of Abramelin, Aradia: Gospel of the Witches, Three Books of Occult Philosophy and the Sworn Book of Honorius, just to name a few. Unlike a Book of Shadows, these tomes are for wider consumption, allowing for spiritual practices and traditions to be created using these well-known grimoires as a foundation.

"Book of Shadows" is a term coined by Gerald Gardner during his creation of Wicca. It was basically Gardner's coven's instruction manual, but over time it has evolved into a highly personal book to record your experiences, ideas, feelings and magical practice. It will likely still have correspondences, spells, rituals, and other bits and pieces of information, but it's tailored to your specific practice. It won't be a generalized book of information with no basis in your personal path. It might be elaborately decorated or kept pretty simple, depending on your preference. There is plenty of scope to make your Book of Shadows as personal to you as you want.

—Stacey Carroll

12 Saturday
Moon ☽ in Cancer ♋

13 Sunday
Moon ☽ in Cancer ♋

February

14 Monday

Moon ○ in Cancer ♋
Moon ○ v/c 5:27 am
Moon ○ enters Leo ♌ 6:17 am
Mercury ☿ enters Aquarius ♒ 4:53 pm

15 Tuesday

Moon ○ in Leo ♌

16 Wednesday

Full Moon ○ in Leo ♌ 11:57 am
Moon ○ v/c 11:57 am
Moon ○ enters Virgo ♍ 3:42 pm

Snow Moon

17 Thursday

Moon ○ in Virgo ♍

18 Friday

Moon ○ in Virgo ♍
Sun ☉ enters Pisces ♓ 11:42 am
Moon ○ v/c 6:20 pm
Moon ○ enters Libra ♎ 10:50 pm

Sun enters Pisces (Water)

Set in Eastern Standard Time (EST)

Using a Pendulum

Pendulums are fantastic divination tools for those who would like a divination method that is both straightforward and insightful. A pendulum is simply a weighted object on the end of a string. If you've visited metaphysical or magical shops, it's likely you've seen a beautiful variety of pendulums; they are commonly made with a pointed crystal on the end of a chain, though some are made with copper or even wood pieces. Pendulums do not need to be fancy or expensive, however—some people have used necklaces as pendants, or even a threaded button.

The diviner can easily begin receiving "yes" or "no" answers by observing the motion of a pendulum. When you are ready to begin working with your pendulum, try the following steps:

1. Rest your elbow on a steady surface as to keep as still as possible. Hold the top of the pendulum's chain or string between your thumb and index finger.
2. In your mind, or out loud, greet the pendulum and thank it for assisting you in clearly and accurately answering questions.
3. Ask the pendulum to show you "YES." Be mindful of the way the pendulum moves, as this is how it will move when it answers "yes" to a question. Next, ask the pendulum to show you "NO." The pendulum will move in a different direction. Finally, ask the pendulum to show you "I DON'T KNOW." Again, observe the motions.
4. Once you've determined how the pendulum communicates its answers, you may begin asking questions. Record the answers so you can reflect on their accuracy at a later time.
5. Close the session by thanking the pendulum.   —*Kiki Dombrowski*

19 Saturday

Moon ○ in Libra ♎

20 Sunday

Moon ☽ in Libra ♎

21 Monday

Moon ☽ in Libra ♎
Moon ☽ v/c 12:02 am
Moon ☽ enters Scorpio ♏ 4:20 am

22 Tuesday

Moon ☽ in Scorpio ♏

23 Wednesday

Moon ☽ v/c 4:24 am
Moon ☽ enters Sagittarius ♐ 8:29 am
Waning Half Moon ☽ 5:32 pm

24 Thursday

Moon ☽ in Sagittarius ♐
Moon ☽ v/c 10:25 pm

25 Friday

Moon ☽ enters Capricorn ♑ 11:28 am

7-Day Spell for a Raise or Promotion

This spell helps you create the necessary self-confidence for upgrading your work life, by sending the message to the Universe that you are worthy of what you're asking for. For best results, work the spell at least one week before approaching your employer.

You will need:
- 1 green or white 7-day candle
- Writing paper
- Parchment paper (optional)
- Envelope

Instructions:
1. Light the candle. Meditate on your positive qualities and brainstorm several self-affirming statements on paper. For example, "I am dependable." "I treat people with courtesy." "I provide valuable service to people." Important: make sure you believe what you're writing! Otherwise, it's unlikely to work. Pick 7 statements that you most resonate with and write them on a new piece of writing or parchment paper.
2. Read the statements out loud, fold the paper in thirds, and place in the envelope. Drip some wax from the candle onto the back of the envelope as a seal. You can also inscribe a symbol in the wax that represents your goal.Then say the following (or similar) words:

   "I know my value, and so do those around me. I know my employer is lucky to have found me. With these words, I affirm my worthiness. With this spell, I ensure my next success. So let it be."
3. Place the envelope on your altar. When you're ready to approach your employer, keep your affirmations in mind. Keep the candle where it can safely burn out on its own. **—Lisa Chamberlain**

---

26 Saturday

Moon ◗ in Capricorn ♑

---

27 Sunday

Moon ◗ in Capricorn ♑
Moon ◗ v/c 9:49 am
Moon ◗ enters Aquarius ♒ 1:36 pm

---

28 Monday

Moon ◑ in Aquarius ≈
Moon ◑ v/c 9:01 pm

1 Tuesday

Moon ◑ enters Pisces ♓ 4:54 pm

2 Wednesday

●

New Moon ● in Pisces ♓ 1:35 pm

3 Thursday

Moon ● in Pisces ♓
Moon ● v/c 5:45 pm
Moon ● enters Aries ♈ 8:53 pm

4 Friday

Moon ◐ in Aries ♈

Claiming Ritual for a New Home

If you're moving, this ritual is a great way to establish a harmonious energy in your new space.

You will need:

- A candle and something to carry it in
- A broom
- Incense
- An offering for the new home (red wine, beer, milk, or water) and two glasses

Instructions:

1. Announce to your previous home that you are moving to a new home. Light the candle and place it in a lantern or jar. Leave through the front door, carrying the flame with you. If you're driving, have another adult hold it for you, or secure it in a cup holder. (If you can't manage this safely, substitute a flameless candle, or another object associated with the hearth, such as a chimney hook.)
2. When you arrive at your new home, carry the flame inside and set it on its new hearth—the mantel if you have a fireplace, or the kitchen stove. Go around the house and open all the windows and doors. Invite any spirits who don't wish to live with you to leave. Sweep all floors, including the threshold at the front door, to purify it. Light incense at the hearth for your hearth spirit, and any other spirits who may choose to stay with you.
3. Pour two glasses of the offering. Toast the home and your new relationship with it. Empty one glass across the threshold, and drink from the second glass. Enjoy being in your new home and feel gratitude for it. The home is a sacred space, the hub of your mundane and spiritual life, and your relationship with it is also sacred.
4. When finished, close the windows and doors and extinguish the candle.

—Heidi Hall

5 Saturday

Moon ☽ in Aries ♈

6 Sunday

Moon ☽ in Aries ♈
Moon ☽ v/c 12:02 am
Mars ♂ enters Aquarius ♒ 2:22 am
Venus ♀ enters Aquarius ♒ 2:29 am
Moon ☽ enters Taurus ♉ 4:00 am

March

7 Monday

Moon ☽ in Taurus ♉

8 Tuesday

Moon ☽ in Taurus ♉
Moon ☽ v/c 10:35 am
Moon ☽ enters Gemini ♊ 2:40 pm

9 Wednesday

Moon ☽ in Gemini ♊
Mercury ☿ enters Pisces ♓ 9:32 pm

10 Thursday

Waxing Half Moon ☽ in Gemini ♊ 6:46 am
Moon ☽ v/c 12:43 pm

11 Friday

Moon ☽ enters Cancer ♋ 3:25 am

Set in Eastern Standard Time (EST)

Morning Reset Mini Ritual

Anchor yourself in the moment with a reset ritual any time of the year. Resetting allows you to take a step back from your stress, worry, or fear and come back stronger and more stabilized, with a new layer of protective energy. This simple mini ritual can be repeated weekly, monthly, or even daily. It's a short ritual meant to be repeated often. If you choose a facial oil, try rosehip, jojoba, apricot kernel, olive, or almond, depending on your preference. Alternatively, you can use your regular moisturizer, or even just water charged for the purpose.

You will need:

- A few drops of facial oil, moisturizer, or charged water

Instructions:

1. Cleanse your hands and tie back your hair from your face.
2. Wash your face and pat dry.
3. If using facial oil or moisturizer, apply to your fingertips and spread evenly over your face.
4. Begin with your forehead. Place your knuckles between your eyebrows and move them upwards towards your hairline. Repeat three times and focus on your intentions, chanting: *"I reset my mind."*
5. Next, move to your eye area and very gently use your ring finger to roll in an oval like circle. Repeat three times, chanting: *"I reset my sight."*
6. Then, move to your cheeks and rest your knuckles near the bridge of the nose. Swipe towards the ears. Repeat three times, chanting: *"I reset my emotions."*
7. Move to your mouth and make a "V" shape with your index and middle finger. Position your index finger above your lip and middle finger below. Press gently and pull towards your ears. Repeat three times on each side of the face then chant: *"I reset my voice."*   **—Ambrosia Hawthorn**

12 Saturday

Moon ☽ in Cancer ♋

13 Sunday

Moon ☽ in Cancer ♋
Moon ☽ v/c 11:44 am
Moon ☽ enters Leo ♌ 3:32 pm

March

14 Monday

Moon ☾ in Leo ♌

15 Tuesday

Moon ☾ in Leo ♌
Moon ☾ v/c 6:56 am

16 Wednesday

Moon ☾ enters Virgo ♍ 12:59 am

17 Thursday

Moon ☾ in Virgo ♍

18 Friday

Full Moon ☾ in Virgo ♍ 3:18 am
Moon ☾ v/c 4:10 am
Moon ☾ enters Libra ♎ 7:26 am

Storm Moon

Ostara: A Time to Grow

Ostara is the Sabbat aligned with the Spring Equinox. It was named for a Germanic goddess (variously spelled as Ostara, Oestra, and Eostra) who was associated with springtime, and for whom the Germanic month of April was named.

Ostara falls between the end of Winter and the high point of Summer. It is the time when the natural world and all within it are experiencing rebirth, new growth and an abundance of greening. The days are reaching their fullness and the nights are becoming shorter and warmer, allowing for more time in our days and in our lives. Ostara is a wonderful time to look at the things you have been working on, acknowledge the progress you've made, and reflect on what you want to grow in your life. It's also a wonderful time to begin creating new plans to reach your goals, and working toward them joyfully.

I adore the Spring Equinox. It is a time where I am most happy in my garden, watching things grow and bloom, and working in concert with my plants to build a strong relationship so that magic carries over into my daily practice. During this time, rituals for fertility, growth, prosperity and new beginnings are definitely the magic to work with. Decorate your altar with eggs, rabbits, daffodils and tulips; indulge in delights of hot cross buns, milk, chocolate, honey and fresh, ripe Spring fruits. Give thanks to the Deities of Spring, to the Greenman and Green Woman. Take the time to paint eggs to symbolize the coming fertility and growth. Set intentions and watch them blossom as you move through Spring.

—Stacey Carroll

19 Saturday

Moon ○ in Libra ♎

20 Sunday

Moon ○ in Libra ♎
Moon ○ v/c 8:39 am
Sun ☉ enters Aries ♈ 11:33 am
Moon ○ enters Scorpio ♏ 11:44 am

Ostara / Spring Equinox 11:33 am

Sun enters Aries (Fire)

March

21 Monday

Moon ☽ in Scorpio ♏

22 Tuesday

Moon ☽ in Scorpio ♏
Moon ☽ v/c 12:01 pm
Moon ☽ enters Sagittarius ♐ 2:59 pm

23 Wednesday

Moon ☽ in Sagittarius ♐

24 Thursday

Moon ☽ in Sagittarius ♐
Moon ☽ v/c 8:59 am
Moon ☽ enters Capricorn ♑ 5:53 pm

25 Friday

Waning Half Moon ☽ in Capricorn ♑ 1:38 am

Egg Shell Symbolism in Magic

Egg shells are a blessed and sacred symbol in spiritual practices. The egg represents birth, rebirth and growth because of the role it plays in nature, but also protection, since the shell offers the protective shield to allow growth to occur. We also use eggs for color correspondences—their natural tones of light blue, browns, grays, greens, and speckles offer connections to tranquility, stability, foundation, and abundance.

Egg shells often come powdered, like cascarilla, or in dried crumbles, but if you're finding them in nature for rituals, there are more elements to consider. An egg that hasn't hatched symbolizes unforeseen setbacks or intentions not manifesting to fruition. Cracked emptied eggs can symbolize growth and movement, since the intention of the egg has manifested. Those with the yolk inside, however, represent symbolic or literal death, lost chances, and poor circumstances.

The birds that the eggs come from also add correspondence. Swallows represent healing, for instance, and have been the subject of many old folk medicine practices. Robin's eggs, known for their vibrant blue tone, represent divinity and rebirth. Researching your particular bird for symbolism before use will guide your use of the egg.

Source these eggs when they've fallen, or when you've watched them for a few months and know they are "empty." When gathered, wash thoroughly. Crush and sprinkle shells around home thresholds for protection, or grind and burn in incense. Often, their presence on the altar is enough for cleansing, growth and "new beginnings" spell work.

—Sarah Justice

---

26 Saturday

Moon ◗ in Capricorn ♑
Moon ◗ v/c 7:51 pm
Moon ◗ enters Aquarius ♒ 8:56 pm

---

27 Sunday

Moon ◗ in Aquarius ♒
Mercury ☿ enters Aries ♈ 3:44 am

March/April

28 Monday

Moon ☽ in Aquarius ≈
Moon ☽ v/c 10:12 am

29 Tuesday

Moon ☽ enters Pisces ♓ 12:31 am

30 Wednesday

Moon ☽ in Pisces ♓

31 Thursday

Moon ● in Pisces ♓
Moon ● v/c 2:36 am
Moon ● enters Aries ♈ 5:31 am

1 Friday

New Moon ● in Aries ♈ 2:25 am

Set in Eastern Daylight Time (EDT)

Simple Seed Blessing

Blessing seeds and fields prior to planting has been a common practice likely since humans began growing crops 10,000 years ago. Farmers had many rituals for ensuring a bountiful crop, since without it, they would not have survived the harsh winters. Today, we have lost our connection to agricultural cycles and the traditions designed to protect crops and increase their yields. You can reconnect to these roots by starting a small garden of your own, whether it's in pots, raised beds, or in the ground!. This seed blessing ritual works for any kind of planting, including indoor seedlings that will go outdoors later in the season.

Instructions:

1. As you plant your seeds, recite the following incantation to encourage hearty growth:

   "Seeds of mine sown with care, A plentiful crop you shall bear.
   May the Sun provide you strength,
   So you may grow to tremendous lengths.
   May the Water to nourish your roots,
   To encourage your flowering and fruits.
   May the Earth feed your tender shoots,
   And allow you to grow deeper roots.
   May the Air give you breath, And prevent an untimely death.
   Together Elements four, Help these seeds I so adore."

2. After the seeds are planted, be sure to give them a drink of water to encourage continued growth. Each time you water, you can recite this same incantation. When the plants bear fruit, leave them an offering as a thank you.   **—Autumn Willow**

---

2 Saturday

Moon ● in Aries ♈
Moon ● v/c 9:52 am
Moon ● enters Taurus ♉ 12:51 pm

---

3 Sunday

Moon ● in Taurus ♉

April

4 Monday

Moon ● in Taurus ♉
Moon ● v/c 9:53 pm
Moon ● enters Gemini ♊ 11:04 pm

5 Tuesday

Moon ● in Gemini ♊
Venus ♀ enters Pisces ♓ 11:17 am

6 Wednesday

Moon ● in Gemini ♊
Moon ● v/c 11:15 pm

7 Thursday

Moon ● enters Cancer ♋ 11:30 am

8 Friday

Moon ● in Cancer ♋

Set in Eastern Daylight Time (EDT)

Good Morning Coffee Spell

Many people love a cup of coffee first thing in the morning. The very fragrance helps us feel more awake and prepared to face the day. Coffee magically corresponds to the Element of Fire and the planet Mars. Because of this, it is can be an ally in empowering your mind and body. The caffeine in coffee is known to stimulate the mind and give energy to the body. Therefore, coffee can support in conjuring courage, inspiration, and awakening opportunities. Coffee has also been used in hex-breaking magic, so consider brewing coffee a simple way to keep negative energy away when you begin your morning. Additionally, you can turn your morning coffee into a small spell to help support you during the day.

You will need:
- Freshly brewed coffee
- Your creamer (or milk) of choice
- Your sweetener of choice
- A spoon
- Your favorite mug

Instructions:
1. Pour the coffee into your mug and say, *"May this coffee awaken me to a bright and beneficial day."* Stir the coffee in a clockwise (deosil) direction three times.
2. Pour in your milk/creamer and say, *"May this creamer allow my day's plans to go smoothly."* Stir the coffee deosil three times.
3. Add your sweetener and say, *"May this sweeten my day with joy and kindness."* Again, stir the coffee deosil three times.
4. Hold the mug in your hand and say, *"I have the energy and willingness to set my intentions and have a good day."* Take a moment to consider what your ideal day will look like. Then, enjoy your cup of coffee!

—Kiki Dombrowski

9 Saturday

Waxing Half Moon ☽ in Cancer ♋ 2:48 am
Moon ☽ v/c 9:01 pm

10 Sunday

Moon ☽ enters Leo ♌ 12:00 am
Mercury ☿ enters Taurus ♉ 10:09 pm

April

11 Monday

Moon ☽ in Leo ♌

12 Tuesday

Moon ☽ in Leo ♌
Moon ☽ v/c 6:17 am
Moon ☽ enters Virgo ♍ 10:08 am

13 Wednesday

Moon ☽ in Virgo ♍

14 Thursday

Moon ☽ in Virgo ♍
Moon ☽ v/c 2:11 pm
Moon ☽ enters Libra ♎ 4:45 pm
Mars ♂ enters Pisces ♓ 11:05 pm

15 Friday

Moon ☽ in Libra ♎

Set in Eastern Daylight Time (EDT)

Nut Butter Esbat Cookies

Craft some magic in your kitchen with Moon Esbat Cookies. They're perfect for ritual offerings or simply sharing with loved ones. They're even fun for the little ones, too! This recipe is for no-bake nut butter cookies that will help you raise energy to achieve your intentions and promote the success of your Moon spells and rituals. To sweeten the recipe, you can mix together sugar and cinnamon to sprinkle cinnamon sugar over the cookies.

You will need:

- 1 cup cashews
- 1 cup pitted Medjool dates
- ½ cup smooth nut butter (almond or peanut)
- 1½ tsps vanilla extract
- Pinch of cacao, cocoa powder, or cinnamon
- Sugar & cinnamon mix (optional)
- Food processor
- Moon-shaped cookie cutter (optional)

Instructions:

1. Gather your ingredients and clear away unwanted energy from your space.
2. Place the cashews, dates, nut butter, and vanilla in the food processor. Blend until mostly smooth.
3. Roll a spoonful of batter into a ball, then flatten with a spoon on a flat surface. Then using a fork, press the tines flat against the batter to create hash marks on the cookies. Or flatten the cookies with your hand and use a moon cookie cutter to create Moon shapes.
4. Sprinkle the cocoa, cacao, or cinnamon over the cookies as you focus on your intention for this recipe.
5. Use these cookies during the cake and ale phase of your Esbat ritual, or enjoy them in observance of the moon as you journal, meditate, or sit under the moonlight.

—Severina Sosa

16 Saturday

Full Moon ○ in Libra ♎ 2:55 pm
Moon ○ v/c 5:57 pm
Moon ○ enters Scorpio ♏ 8:23 pm

Pink Moon

17 Sunday

Moon ○ in Scorpio ♏

April

18 Monday

Moon ☽ in Scorpio ♏
Moon ☽ v/c 7:55 pm
Moon ☽ enters Sagittarius ♐ 10:17 pm

19 Tuesday

Moon ☽ in Sagittarius ♐
Sun ☉ enters Taurus ♉ 10:24 pm

Sun enters Taurus (Earth)

20 Wednesday

Moon ☽ in Sagittarius ♐
Moon ☽ v/c 4:56 pm
Moon ☽ enters Capricorn ♑ 11:52 pm

21 Thursday

Moon ☽ in Capricorn ♑

22 Friday

Moon ☽ in Capricorn ♑
Moon ☽ v/c 11:53 pm

Inviting the House Serpent Into Your Home

The House Serpent is a type of house spirit connected with health and wealth in the home, most often found in northern European traditions. Before the Christianization of Europe, snakes didn't have the negative associations that they do now, especially when it came to non-venomous and non-aggressive snakes. Instead, snakes were regarded as symbols of fertility and abundance, and even as the reincarnations of the ancestors. Grass snakes were seen as guardians of the cattle and contributors to the fertility of the soil. They were welcomed in people's homes, and seen as physical representatives of the House Serpent, or the genius locii of the home and its surrounding land. In The Tradition of Household Spirits, Claude Lecouteux writes that "the snake... is one of the most ancient forms" that house spirits take.

To invite a House Serpent into your home, the ritual is simple:

You will need:

- Milk and bread
- A candle (optional)

Instructions:

1. Place the milk and bread on the hearth, or on the floor in front of the stove, just before bedtime. Recite this rhyme, taken from the Brothers Grimm's "Stories About Snakes":
   "Snake, snake, come swiftly, Hither come, thou tiny thing,
   Thou shalt have thy crumbs of bread, Thou shalt refresh thyself with milk."
2. Leave it overnight and dispose of it in the morning.
3. If you ever come across a grass, black rat, or corn snake in or around your home, do not kill it. It is taboo to do so and will offend the House Serpent. Repeat this ritual at certain times of the year—every full moon, or on holidays—to maintain a good relationship with this house spirit.

—Heidi Hall

23 Saturday

Moon ☽ enters Aquarius ♒ 2:17 am
Waning Half Moon ☽ 7:56 am

24 Sunday

Moon ☽ in Aquarius ♒
Moon ☽ v/c 8:34 pm

25 Monday

Moon ◐ enters Pisces ♓ 6:15 am

26 Tuesday

Moon ◐ in Pisces ♓

27 Wednesday

Moon ◐ in Pisces ♓
Moon ◐ v/c 9:35 am
Moon ◐ enters Aries ♈ 12:10 pm

28 Thursday

Moon ● in Aries ♈

29 Friday

Moon ● in Aries ♈
Pluto ♇ ℞ 2:36 pm
Moon ● v/c 5:39 pm
Mercury ☿ enters Gemini ♊ 6:22 pm
Moon ● enters Taurus ♉ 8:19 pm

68   *Set in Eastern Daylight Time (EDT)*

Beltane Flowers

One of the most delightful traditions at Beltane is the weaving and wearing of flower crowns. It's a great way to connect with Nature and beautify yourself for this playful Sabbat!

The ideal crown is made from wildflowers gathered outdoors on Beltane day, but you can also work with a purchased bouquet—just dry the stems as much as possible before you begin.

There are plenty of tutorials for making flower crowns online. Many use wire and glue to make the base of the crown, but you can also go the old-fashioned route and use nothing but the flowers themselves! Be sure to leave the stems as long as possible when you pick them, as they will be forming your base. (Avoid flowers with tough or thorny stems, and check under stems and leaves to avoid disturbing any insects.) Once you've braided the base, you can tuck in shorter-stemmed flowers.

If you want, you can tailor your crown for specific magical purposes. Any wildflowers growing near you will be magically potent for your Beltane celebrations, but here are a few correspondences to get you started:

Buttercup: *love, commitment, fertility, fidelity, humility*
Columbine: *love, feminine power, beauty, courage*
Clover: *good luck, love, protection, prosperity, faerie magic*
Daisy: *youthful energy, joy, love, flirtation, baby blessings*
Dandelion: *divination, interaction with the spirit world, wishes*
Honeysuckle: *intuition, psychic ability, prosperity, love, luck*
Hyacinth: *love, joy, wishes, clearing negativity*
Violet: *protection, love, restful sleep, tranquility, harmony, luck*

You can dry the flowers from your crown after Beltane for use in future spells or altar decorations. —*Lisa Chamberlain*

30 Saturday

New Moon ● in Taurus ♉ 4:28 pm

Solar Eclipse 4:27 pm – 10° Tau ♉ 28'

1 Sunday

Moon ● in Taurus ♉

Beltane

May

2 Monday

Moon ● in Taurus ♉
Moon ● v/c 6:13 am
Moon ● enters Gemini ♊ 6:47 am
Venus ♀ enters Aries ♈ 12:10 pm

3 Tuesday

Moon ● in Gemini ♊

4 Wednesday

Moon ● in Gemini ♊
Moon ● v/c 4:37 pm
Moon ● enters Cancer ♋ 7:05 pm

5 Thursday

Moon ● in Cancer ♋

6 Friday

Moon ◑ in Cancer ♋

Beltane cross-quarter day 08:25 am

Set in Eastern Daylight Time (EDT)

How to Use Loose Incense

Loose incense, while more complex than stick or cone incense, can add a nice traditional ambience to your ritual and spellwork.

You can buy pre-blended loose incense or create your own. If you like a mostly resinous incense blend, then a combination of frankincense, myrrh, copal or benzoin will provide a strong scent. Adding herbs makes the incense go further and allows for more flexibility in creating a customized blend. For best results let a homemade blend sit for a few days to marinate and combine (but if you want to use it right away, that's perfectly okay).

To burn loose incense you'll need a lit charcoal disc; these are available at many different new age stores and online. You also need a heatproof dish, such as ceramic, cast iron (like a small cauldron), or even a terra-cotta pot base. On the dish, place a heatproof material such as sand or salt to absorb some of the heat from your charcoal disc.

Hold the disc with a pair of small tongs and light it. The disc will spark as you do this. Place it on your heatproof surface and allow the disc to turn completely grey. Once grey, it is hot and ready for use.

Sprinkle your loose incense over the lit disc. A word of caution: more is not merrier in this scenario. If you put too much on, you will smother the disc and it will become very smoky. Add a little bit at a time and it will burn evenly, creating a light smoke. Simply add your blend as needed and allow it to burn.

—Stacey Carroll

7 Saturday

Moon ◖ in Cancer ♋
Moon ◖ v/c 6:26 am
Moon ◖ enters Leo ♌ 7:50 am

8 Sunday

Waxing Half Moon ◖ in Leo ♌ 8:22 pm

May

9 Monday

Moon ☽ in Leo ♌
Moon ☽ v/c 8:38 am
Moon ☽ enters Virgo ♍ 6:53 pm

10 Tuesday

Moon ☽ in Virgo ♍
Mercury ☿ ℞ 7:47 am
Jupiter ♃ enters Aries ♈ 7:21 pm

Mercury retrograde until June 3

11 Wednesday

Moon ☽ in Virgo ♍

12 Thursday

Moon ☽ in Virgo ♍
Moon ☽ v/c 12:00 am
Moon ☽ enters Libra ♎ 2:35 am

13 Friday

Moon ☽ in Libra ♎

Lunar Eclipse Superstitions and Magic

Lunar eclipses occur when the Earth moves between the Moon and the Sun. The Earth casts a shadow onto the Moon, making it take on a dark, reddish hue. These lunar occasions are associated with some interesting superstitions from around the world.

Tibetan Buddhists believe that your actions, good or bad, are multiplied tenfold during an eclipse. In India, people avoid cooking, eating, and drinking during the lunar eclipse because of a belief that the eclipse quickly spoils food. Ancient Incas believed that a mythological jaguar in the sky was attacking the moon during a lunar eclipse. In an attempt to scare away the jaguar, Incas would shake their spears at the heavens and make their dogs bark at the moon. A tribe in the Benin and Togo nations of western Africa say that the Sun and Moon are fighting during the eclipse. During this time, they make prayers for the two celestial bodies to find resolution. The reddish hue of the lunar eclipse has also been seen as an omen of harm, and some people believe that wounds suffered during an eclipse will not heal properly.

Modern day Witches and magical practitioners see the lunar eclipse as a time where psychic abilities feel heightened. In light of some of the superstitions discussed above, we can consider some of the following magical work to focus on during lunar eclipses:

1. Use meditation and prayer
   to work through internal conflicts that need resolution.
2. Practice magic to banish the metaphorical monsters that are trying to "swallow you."
3. Perform healing rituals to support wellness and safe transitions.
4. Celebrate the cycles of life and honor lunar deities.

—Kiki Dombrowski

14 Saturday

Moon ○ in Libra ♎
Moon ○ v/c 4:07 am
Moon ○ enters Scorpio ♏ 6:33 am

15 Sunday

Moon ○ in Scorpio ♏

May

16 Monday

Full Moon ○ in Scorpio ♏ 12:15 am
Moon ○ v/c 5:29 am
Moon ○ enters Sagittarius ♐ 7:51 am

Lunar Eclipse 12:13 am – 25° Sco♏ 18'

Flower Moon

17 Tuesday

Moon ○ in Sagittarius ♐

18 Wednesday

Moon ◑ in Sagittarius ♐
Moon ◑ v/c 12:00 am
Moon ◑ enters Capricorn ♑ 8:01 am

19 Thursday

Moon ◑ in Capricorn ♑

20 Friday

Moon ◑ in Capricorn ♑
Moon ◑ v/c 8:00 am
Moon ◑ enters Aquarius ♒ 8:53 am
Sun ☉ enters Gemini ♊ 9:22 pm

Sun enters Gemini (Air)

Dreamweaver Tea

Dream recall is an invaluable form of divination, offering insight into what the future holds. However, not everyone can easily remember their dreams, and some people claim to not dream at all! Dream recall is a skill that must be honed through dedicated journaling right when you wake up, but there are a host of spells, crystals, and teas that can make the experience easier. This particular tea is designed to help you relax, to promote dreaming, and to aid in dream recall.

You will need:

- 1 teaspoon dried chamomile
- 1 teaspoon dried lavender
- 1 teaspoon dried lemon balm
- 1 teaspoon dried oat straw
- 1 teaspoon dried passionflower
- 1 teaspoon dried mugwort

Instructions:

Combine the herbs into a small bowl and mix gently but thoroughly. Store in an airtight, glass container until you are ready to use.

I suggest using this tea for 7 days straight if you are a beginner, preferably starting on the New Moon. Keep a journal and writing utensil next to your bed and as soon as you wake up, start recording everything you can remember, even if it doesn't make sense or the details are slim. Over time, your recall will improve so the memories flow freely. I encourage you not to try and interpret your dreams at this time until you are able to recall more details. If you have a moment during your day, read through what you wrote in the morning and see if any more information comes to you. Make note of anything else you remember, feelings you have, or messages you receive. This will help you understand your dreams and make accurate interpretations down the road.   *—Autumn Willow*

---

21   Saturday

Moon ☽ in Aquarius ♒

---

22   Sunday

Moon ☽ in Aquarius ♒
Moon ☽ v/c 3:20 am
Moon ☽ enters Pisces ♓ 11:49 am
Waning Half Moon ☽ 2:43 pm
Mercury ☿ enters Taurus ♉ 9:14 pm

May

23 Monday

Moon ☽ in Pisces ♓

24 Tuesday

Moon ☽ in Pisces ♓
Moon ☽ v/c 5:34 pm
Moon ☽ enters Aries ♈ 5:40 pm
Mars ♂ enters Aries ♈ 7:17 pm

25 Wednesday

Moon ☽ in Aries ♈

26 Thursday

Moon ☽ in Aries ♈
Moon ☽ v/c 11:20 pm

27 Friday

Moon ☽ enters Taurus ♉ 2:23 am

Bell Spell for New Beginnings

Bells have been used for thousands of years to cleanse and protect spaces, as well as to call upon spirits. Bells are also linked to fresh starts by way of Elemental correspondences: they are a ritual tool for the element of Air, which deals with clearing out old energies to make way for new beginnings. Furthermore, Air corresponds to the eastern direction, which also symbolizes newness. Because of such strong correspondences, we can use bells in spell work for cleansing and encouraging healthy new beginnings.

This bell spell helps to manifest positivity as you begin a new journey, or to cleanse your energy to make way for growth.

You will need:

- 9 bells
- 2 feet (60 cm) of twine
- Other strands of textiles, like ribbons or silks that are white, blue, green or gray (optional)

Instructions:

1. Place nine bells of equal distance apart on a sturdy strand of twine. As you tie on each, state the corresponding line:

"The first bell chimes, and as it does, the east winds start to rise. The second rings, and with it brings, the time to wake the eyes. By bell of three, I honor self, and a gentle breeze ensues. Bell of four, which brings support, to join in as air moves. The fifth is strung; it has begun. The winds pick up their speed. By bell of six, the dark winds drift and with it comes reprieve. Bell of seven, the gale force comes and ushers in the change. Eight then nine, by way of divine, the path to change is paved."

2. Consider adding feathers as you tie the bells to add to the Air correspondence.

—Sarah Justice

28 Saturday

Moon ● in Taurus ♉
Venus ♀ enters Taurus ♉ 10:45 am

29 Sunday

Moon ● in Taurus ♉
Moon ● v/c 10:11 am
Moon ● enters Gemini ♊ 1:23 pm

30 Monday

New Moon ● in Gemini ♊ 7:31 am

31 Tuesday

Moon ● in Gemini ♊
Moon ● v/c 4:10 pm

1 Wednesday

Moon ● enters Cancer ♋ 1:49 am

2 Thursday

Moon ● in Cancer ♋

3 Friday

Moon ● in Cancer ♋
Mercury ☿ D 4:00 am
Moon ● v/c 11:15 am
Moon ● enters Leo ♌ 2:38 pm

Mercury direct

Protection Necklace Amulet

Fortify your defenses by turning your personal jewelry into a protective amulet that can increase your body's own protective defensive energy against unwanted external forces. This spell uses the shielding properties of the color black as well as the protective herb, cumin.

Necklaces that work well as amulets include crystals or metal pendants on a leather cord or chain. Keep comfort in mind when choosing a necklace intended to be worn all times. You can amplify the spell by passing your necklace through the cumin and rinsing it afterward, though this isn't ideal for jewelry that may rust.

To boost your power, combine this spell with the full or waning moon for added protection. You can also charge the item further under the moonlight after the initial spell.

You will need:
- 1 tsp cumin
- Plate (ideally black)
- Black spell candle
- Necklace

Instructions:
1. Gather your materials and cleanse your necklace.
2. Light your candle and set your intentions for protection.
3. Lay your necklace in the center of the plate.
4. Sprinkle the cumin in a circle around the necklace.
5. Pass your hand clockwise over the cumin and say:
"I imbue this necklace with my intention, Charge with protection from any direction."
6. Allow your energy to infuse with the necklace to create your charged amulet as the candle burns down.
7. When the candle has gone out on its own, put on your amulet. Rinse and put away the plate. Re-charge the necklace every few weeks.

—Ambrosia Hawthorn

4 Saturday

Moon ◑ in Leo ♌
Saturn ♄ ℞ 5:47 pm

5 Sunday

Moon ◑ in Leo ♌
Moon ◑ v/c 7:12 pm

June

6   Monday

Moon ☽ enters Virgo ♍ 2:22 am

7   Tuesday

Waxing Half Moon ☽ in Virgo ♍ 10:49 am

8   Wednesday

Moon ☽ in Virgo ♍
Moon ☽ v/c 8:09 am
Moon ☽ enters Libra ♎ 11:22 am

9   Thursday

Moon ☽ in Libra ♎

10   Friday

Moon ☽ in Libra ♎
Moon ☽ v/c 1:36 pm
Moon ☽ enters Scorpio ♏ 4:41 pm

Set in Eastern Daylight Time (EDT)

Charm Bag for Deterring Unwanted Attention

Many of us sometimes wish for the superpower of invisibility. This deflecting spell is a good real-world alternative.

You will need:

- A candle and incense
- A piece of cloth and some twine for tying it into a sachet
- Warding herbs, such as wormwood, peppermint, lavender, rue, lemon balm, or marigold
- A small piece or two of bramble or rose stem
- A few small pieces of reflective metal to deflect the unwanted attention

Instructions:

1. Light the candle and incense. Take a moment or two to ground yourself in your space. Open up inside, becoming more sensitive to your environment and to the items in front of you, each with their own spirits. Greet them silently with a simple feeling of acknowledgement and gratitude.
2. One by one, place the items in the center of the cloth. As you touch them, state the powers you'd like them to contribute to this charm bag. When all the items are on the cloth, place your hand over them. Feel the threads of energy they radiate and slowly rotate your hand clockwise above them, as if you are twisting and binding those energies together.
3. When the work feels complete, bind up the cloth into a little bag or sachet by pulling the edges together and tying it securely with twine. Then hold the bag over the incense smoke to feed the spirits inside. Feed the spirits this way once a week, or however often seems needed.
4. When you are done, extinguish the candle. Carry the sachet with you on your person or in a bag.   *—Heidi Hall*

11 Saturday

Moon ○ in Scorpio ♏

12 Sunday

Moon ○ in Scorpio ♏
Moon ○ v/c 5:39 pm
Moon ○ enters Sagittarius ♐ 6:31 pm

June

13 Monday

Moon ○ in Sagittarius ♐
Mercury ☿ enters Gemini ♊ 11:26 am

14 Tuesday

○

Full Moon ○ in Sagittarius ♐ 7:51 am
Moon ○ v/c 10:59 am
Moon ○ enters Capricorn ♑ 6:14 pm

Strawberry Moon

15 Wednesday

Moon ○ in Capricorn ♑

16 Thursday

Moon ○ in Capricorn ♑
Moon ○ v/c 2:41 pm
Moon ○ enters Aquarius ♒ 5:44 pm

17 Friday

Moon ○ in Aquarius ♒

Set in Eastern Daylight Time (EDT)

Which Candle to Use?

There are many different types of candles you can use in ritual and spellwork. This rundown of the most common types of candles and their average burn times can help you decide what will work best for your purpose.

Jar: Jar candles are tall, glass-encased candles that can burn for up to 7 days. They are most often used as devotional candles, or in spells and rituals that need a longer working time.

Pillar: Pillar candles are tall, solid, and usually round, but also come in squares, triangles and oval shapes. Pillars are typically made from paraffin, but you can find them in other waxes. Pillars have a long burn time ranging anywhere from 12–100 hours, depending on size, wick, ambient temperature and wax type.

Votive: Votive candles are between a tealight and pillar. They often have a burn time of over 9 hours, but are not as tall as pillars. They can come in a variety of scents and colors.

Tealight: Tealight candles come in small, round metal containers and have a burn time of 4-9 hours. Tealights are convenient for ritual use; they burn long enough to last through ritual but not so long that you have to remain with them for hours afterward. These also come in a range of colors and scents.

Taper: Taper candles will burn for 3+ hours on average. They are most often used as dinner candles, but can be used for many different rituals and spellwork requiring a somewhat longer burn time.

Birthday: Awesome for very quick spellwork, these burn very fast and come in a range of colors and textures.   —*Stacey Carroll*

---

18 Saturday

Moon ☽ in Aquarius ♒
Moon ☽ v/c 2:50 pm
Moon ☽ enters Pisces ♓ 7:01 pm

---

19 Sunday

Moon ☽ in Pisces ♓

20 Monday

Waning Half Moon ☽ in Pisces ♓ 11:10 pm
Moon ☽ v/c 11:10 pm
Moon ☽ enters Aries ♈ 11:36 pm

21 Tuesday

Moon ☽ in Aries ♈
Sun ☉ enters Cancer ♋ 5:13 am

Litha / Summer Solstice 5:14 am

Sun enters Cancer (Water)

22 Wednesday

Moon ☽ in Aries ♈
Venus ♀ enters Gemini ♊ 8:34 pm

23 Thursday

Moon ☽ in Aries ♈
Moon ☽ v/c 4:03 am
Moon ☽ enters Taurus ♉ 7:58 am

24 Friday

Moon ☽ in Taurus ♉

Litha Sunrise Blessing for Joy and Happiness with St. John's Wort

St. John's wort is a bright herb commonly associated with the Summer Solstice. It was named after St. John the Baptist, whose birthday is celebrated on June 24th in the Catholic church. In Medieval Europe, St. John's wort was believed to protect against illness and evil. It was also said that sleeping with St. John's wort under your pillow at the Summer Solstice would encourage dreams of your future beloved. St. John's wort can be used for protection, purification, and promoting happiness in magical work. This simple sunrise blessing will help grow joy and happiness in your life.

You will need:

- Honey
- St. John's wort flowers (fresh or dried)
- Fresh summer flowers (e.g., daisies, chamomile, yarrow, or lilac)
- A piece of sunstone or amber
- A decorative dish

1. Prior to sunrise, arrange the flowers and honey on the dish in a pattern resembling a sun. Place the crystal in the center. Find a private place to watch the sunrise or perform this at home, facing East.
2. As the Sun begins to rise, say the following: *"As the Sun rises, so does my joy. As the Sun grows, so does my hope. May the Sun guide me towards happiness."* Repeat three times.
3. Hold up the dish and say: *"May this sweet offering bring fortunate blessings into my life and the lives of those I love. Blessings to the Sun. Blessings of joy."*
4. Leave the offering dish in the sunlight for the day. Dispose of the biodegradable offerings in your garden or bury them. Carry the crystal whenever you need an extra boost of happiness, good luck, or the Sun's bright energy.

—Kiki Dombrowski

25 Saturday

Moon ☽ in Taurus ♉
Moon ☽ v/c 3:03 pm
Moon ☽ enters Gemini ♊ 7:14 pm

26 Sunday

Moon ☽ in Gemini ♊

27 Monday

Moon ● in Gemini ♊
Moon ● v/c 10:39 pm

28 Tuesday   ●

Neptune ♆ ℞ 3:55 am
Moon ● enters Cancer ♋ 7:54 am
New Moon ● 10:53 pm

29 Wednesday

Moon ● in Cancer ♋

30 Thursday

Moon ● in Cancer ♋
Moon ● v/c 4:14 pm
Moon ● enters Leo ♌ 8:39 pm

1 Friday

Moon ● in Leo ♌

Runic Goal Setting Spread

When we're wanting a lot out of life, sometimes it can feel impossible to figure out where to start. Goal setting is a great way to improve your spiritual practice and your daily life, as it helps you focus on an achievable end result. This runic spread can help you decide out what goals are best for you to set at this time, and what you will need to do to achieve those goals. It's based on a SMART goal format: Specific, Measurable, Achievable, Realistic, and Timely. This spread is ideal to use during the New or Waxing Moon.

You will need:

• Set of Runes

Instructions:

Set up your sacred space and randomly draw 5 runes placing them in the layout below:

1. What Specific goal should I focus on?
2. What Measurable steps must I take to meet this goal?
3. What will be the results of this Achievement?
4. What must I release to make this goal Realistic?
5. How much Time will it take to meet this goal?

If anything about the reading is unclear, draw a clarifying rune.

—Autumn Willow

---

2 Saturday

Moon ◐ in Leo ♌

---

3 Sunday

Moon ◐ in Leo ♌
Moon ◐ v/c 5:59 am
Moon ◐ enters Virgo ♍ 8:31 am

July

4 Monday

Moon ☽ in Virgo ♍

5 Tuesday

Moon ☽ in Virgo ♍
Mars ♂ enters Taurus ♉ 2:03 am
Mercury ☿ enters Cancer ♋ 2:24 am
Moon ☽ v/c 2:04 pm
Moon ☽ enters Libra ♎ 6:24 pm

6 Wednesday

Waxing Half Moon ☽ in Libra ♎ 10:15 pm

7 Thursday

Moon ☽ in Libra ♎
Moon ☽ v/c 9:04 pm

8 Friday

Moon ☽ enters Scorpio ♏ 1:14 am

Elemental Magic: Earthing

You probably already know that Witches use various grounding techniques to balance their energy, especially after ritual and magical work. One of the simplest methods is to sit, stand, or walk barefoot on the literal ground. Contact with the Earth's surface allows excess energy to be drawn out of our bodies and absorbed into the soil. But did you know that a regular practice of grounding in this manner can have physical health benefits as well?

Many indigenous cultures have always known this. Today, some people in Afghanistan still practice the tradition of walking barefoot on wet grass in the spring to ensure good health. The Hadzabe people of Tanzania, who have largely resisted assimilating into Western culture and spend their days walking, sitting, and sleeping on the ground, have better health than most other rural Africans.

Modern science is also beginning to catch on to the power of the Earth. Studies have shown that Earthing/grounding can positively affect cardiovascular disease, improve respiratory and pulse rates, reduce stress, tension, and inflammation, and improve sleep.

Summer is the perfect time to explore Earthing for yourself. Set aside 15-30 minutes per day for a week, and take note of any differences in how you feel after 7 days. You can sit, stand, or walk—just make sure your bare feet are on the Earth. You can make a ritual out of it if you like, but you can also just trust Earth's magic to work for you, no wands or words required!

Check out the book *Earthing* by Clinton Ober for more information on the health benefits of grounding regularly.

—Lisa Chamberlain

9 Saturday

Moon ☽ in Scorpio ♏

10 Sunday

Moon ☽ in Scorpio ♏
Moon ☽ v/c 12:34 am
Moon ☽ enters Sagittarius ♐ 4:35 am

11 Monday

Moon ○ in Sagittarius ♐
Moon ○ v/c 9:42 pm

12 Tuesday

Moon ○ enters Capricorn ♑ 5:01 am

13 Wednesday

Full Moon ○ in Capricorn ♑ 2:38 pm

Thunder Moon

14 Thursday

Moon ○ in Capricorn ♑
Moon ○ v/c 12:16 am
Moon ○ enters Aquarius ♒ 4:14 am

15 Friday

Moon ○ in Aquarius ♒

Mushroom Grounding Spell

The mushroom is strongly linked to witchcraft and magick. Mushrooms' mysterious reputation stems in part from their seemingly magical ability to appear out of nowhere overnight. The psychotropic nature of some mushrooms has been linked to the notorious Flying Ointment witches anointed their broomsticks with to ride to sabbat meetings. A naturally occurring circle of mushrooms is called a fairy ring, a space where fairies and witches are said to dance.

We can use this link to both witchcraft and the Earth Element in spells concerning grounding. Grounding is the act of returning to the center of self in moments of emotional upheaval, which spellwork can bring. It's also a way to return to the body after rituals with a lot of visualization and meditation, while keeping the body connected to the Universe.

For this spell, dry and grind chanterelle, lion's mane and blue oyster mushrooms together. (Add wood ear mushroom for a bit of love.) As you work, say:

"The Sun drifts in to signal day. The Moon slips round the arc. A celestial dance, archaic prance, one where Earth's the star. For Father brings the growth of things, the sustenance that is real. But Moon's the will to carry them home, and turn them into meal. The Father bestows the light to see, to avoid an ill-fated call; but it's Mother, the dreamer, who guides by the soul to ensure no curses befall. A match of odds, like beach and sod, but the partnership's roots flow deep. It runs like a river deep in the inner, a partnership, too, in me."

Place the dried mushroom blend on a charcoal brick and burn.

—Sarah Justice

16 Saturday

Moon ☽ in Aquarius ♒
Moon ☽ v/c 12:37 am
Moon ☽ enters Pisces ♓ 4:17 am

17 Sunday

Moon ☽ in Pisces ♓
Venus ♀ enters Cancer ♋ 9:32 pm

July

18 Monday

Moon ☽ in Pisces ♓
Moon ☽ v/c 2:43 am
Moon ☽ enters Aries ♈ 7:18 am

19 Tuesday

Moon ☽ in Aries ♈
Mercury ☿ enters Leo ♌ 8:34 am

20 Wednesday

Waning Half Moon ☽ in Aries ♈ 10:19 am
Moon ☽ v/c 10:19 am
Moon ☽ enters Taurus ♉ 2:23 pm

21 Thursday

Moon ☽ in Taurus ♉

22 Friday

Moon ☽ in Taurus ♉
Sun ☉ enters Leo ♌ 4:06 pm
Moon ☽ v/c 7:45 pm

Sun enters Leo (Fire)

Set in Eastern Daylight Time (EDT)

The Element of Fire

Fire: it is both beautiful and dangerous, healing and destructive, warming and terrifying. It is fluid, flexible, fast-changing and explosive. There is a reason candle magic is one of the best and quickest forms—fire is powerful and gets things done.

Those born under the element of Fire (Aries, Leo and Sagittarius) would know how this energy can either work through you for your highest good or be your worst trait. I was born under Fire: my natal chart holds fire in Sun and Rising, and my hair is even fiery, so it's an element I feel a strong affinity for. Working with fire is a wonderful thing, and there are many ways to embrace the energy of the element of Fire in your practice.

Fire is ruled by Mars, Summer and Noon. Its direction is South in the Northern Hemisphere and North in the Southern Hemisphere. It glows colors of red, yellow, white, and orange, and in rare cases, a very distinct blue. Fiery chili, cayenne, ginger, curry, cumin, saffron and cinnamon are associated herbs and spices, while bloodstone, garnet, red jasper and carnelian hold the energy of fire within their hearts.

Work with the elemental energies of salamanders, dragons and the phoenix to give extra punch to your workings. Ask Pele, Prometheus, Haesphaestus or Sekhmet to bless your work and add strength. Embrace energy, will, courage and action to channel Fire through your spirit and into the world. Like recognizes like, so holding the Spirit of Fire within you will bring fast-acting results and a stronger relationship to the element of Fire.

—*Stacey Carroll*

23 Saturday

Moon ◗ enters Gemini ♊ 1:10 am

24 Sunday

Moon ◗ in Gemini ♊

July

25 Monday

Moon ☽ in Gemini ♊
Moon ☽ v/c 4:15 am
Moon ☽ enters Cancer ♋ 1:54 pm

26 Tuesday

Moon ☽ in Cancer ♋

27 Wednesday

Moon ☽ in Cancer ♋
Moon ☽ v/c 8:55 pm

28 Thursday

Moon ☽ enters Leo ♌ 2:36 am
New Moon ● 1:55 pm
Jupiter ♃ ℞ 4:38 pm

29 Friday

Moon ☽ in Leo ♌

Bedtime Bitters Brew

Craft your own herbal bedtime bitters to connect with nature and promote peaceful sleep. This bedtime tincture is made with alcohol, but you can substitute with food-grade vegetable glycerin to make a glycerite, or use apple cider vinegar and honey to make an oxymel.

You will need:

- 1 pint Mason jar
- ½ cup dried motherwort
- 2 tablespoons chamomile flowers
- 2 tablespoons dried spearmint leaves
- 1 cup 100-proof distilled alcohol, such as vodka
- Strainer or cheese cloth
- Funnel
- Labeling materials
- Mortar and pestle
- Bowl
- Dropper bottles

Instructions:

1. Cleanse your space and prepare your ingredients.
2. Using a mortar and pestle or a spice grinder, coarsely grind the herbs.
3. Transfer the herbs into the Mason jar and then cover with the alcohol.
4. Seal the jar, label it, and set your intentions as you turn the closed jar upside down in your hands.
5. Turn the jar upright and place in a cupboard away from sunlight and heat, shaking it daily for 3-4 weeks.
6. Strain the tincture through the cheesecloth into a bowl. Squeeze the cloth to release as much of the liquid as possible, discarding the solids.
7. Pour the tincture through a funnel into a bottle, then seal it with an eyedropper or another tight-fitting plastic lid.
8. Take 5 to 15 drops by mouth before bed for peaceful sleep .

—Severina Sosa

---

30 Saturday

Moon ● in Leo ♌
Moon ● v/c 12:30 am
Moon ● enters Virgo ♍ 2:11 pm

---

31 Sunday

Moon ● in Virgo ♍

August

1 Monday

Moon ☽ in Virgo ♍
Moon ☽ v/c 6:30 pm

Lammas

2 Tuesday

Moon ☽ enters Libra ♎ 12:06 am

3 Wednesday

Moon ☽ in Libra ♎

4 Thursday

Moon ☽ in Libra ♎
Moon ☽ v/c 2:20 am
Mercury ☿ enters Virgo ♍ 2:57 am
Moon ☽ enters Scorpio ♏ 7:47 am

5 Friday

Waxing Half Moon ☽ in Scorpio ♏ 7:07 am

Set in Eastern Daylight Time (EDT)

Lammas Blackberry Long-Term Abundance Spell

I have fond memories of picking blackberries with my grandmother in late summer and baking them into delicious pies, jams, and cookies. Blackberry plants are extremely hardy, fast growing, abundant in their fruit production, and produce large numbers of seeds per berry. A single plant quickly turns into many as they drop new seeds and extend shoots underground. Before you know it, they can take over a large patch of your yard! These traits make blackberry the perfect plant and fruit for long-lasting abundance spells. In this spell, you will plant the seeds for future and continued successes, so pick a place where you don't mind blackberries popping up. While these can be grown in a container, the spell is best planted in the ground.

Six is the number of abundance and is guaranteed to bring riches, hence the use of six blackberries in this spell. Note that this spell takes time and commitment to maintain: the resulting plant won't produce berries in the first year.

You will need:
- 6 blackberries
- Water

Instructions:
Go to the location where you wish to plant your blackberries and dig a small hole, no more than 1–2 inches deep. Place the berries in the same hole and say, *"Blackberries, dark and sweet, bring me much to eat. Bless me with good health, and bring me abundant wealth."* Cover the berries and give them an offering of water. Return often to water your intentions. As the blackberries sprout and grow, so shall your abundance. Remember, if you are lax in your commitment, the spell will suffer. And always remember to thank the plant for the fruit you harvest from it. —*Autumn Willow*

---

6 Saturday

Moon ☽ in Scorpio ♏
Moon ☽ v/c 7:24 am
Moon ☽ enters Sagittarius ♐ 12:38 pm

---

7 Sunday

Moon ☽ in Sagittarius ♐

Lammas cross-quarter day 8:36 am

August

8 Monday

Moon ☽ in Sagittarius ♐
Moon ☽ v/c 6:31 am
Moon ☽ enters Capricorn ♑ 2:38 pm

9 Tuesday

Moon ☽ in Capricorn ♑

10 Wednesday

Moon ☽ in Capricorn ♑
Moon ☽ v/c 12:40 pm
Moon ☽ enters Aquarius ♒ 2:44 pm

11 Thursday

Moon ○ in Aquarius ♒
Venus ♀ in Leo ♌ 2:29 pm
Full Moon ○ 9:36 pm

Corn Moon

12 Friday

Moon ○ in Aquarius ♒
Moon ○ v/c 7:07 am
Moon ○ enters Pisces ♓ 2:45 pm

Tuesday Tarot Message Ritual

This short, routine Tarot reading is perfect for answering frequent questions and providing messages for each week. Tuesdays are associated with Mars and the properties of action, creativity, and confidence. For enhancing your divination abilities, light a white or purple candle. And for assistance directing your energy, use a wand. These are optional tools to power your readings. (You can also substitute another divination method. Oracle decks, rune stones, ogham staves, or any form of scrying can be used.)

For each question, you'll want to reshuffle the cards. Decide whether to pull one card, for a very quick message, or three cards, for a bit more detail.

You will need:
- Candle (optional)
- Wand (optional)
- Tarot deck
- Paper and pen

Instructions:
1. Gather your materials and cleanse your sacred space.
2. Light the candle (if using) and shuffle your Tarot deck, focusing on your question.
3. Fan out the cards and lay them in front of you.
4. Direct your wand (if using) over the fanned-out cards to assist in directing your energy.
5. Pull one or three cards and place them face up.
6. Note the imagery, symbolism, and interpretations of each card.
7. Write down the question you asked, and any impressions you get from the cards. Spend a few moments reflecting on the messages you've received. —*Ambrosia Hawthorn*

13   Saturday
Moon ☽ in Pisces ♓

14   Sunday
Moon ☽ in Pisces ♓
Moon ☽ v/c 11:10 am
Moon ☽ enters Aries ♈ 4:43 pm

15 Monday

Moon ☽ in Aries ♈

---

16 Tuesday

Moon ☽ in Aries ♈
Moon ☽ v/c 4:18 pm
Moon ☽ enters Taurus ♉ 10:23 pm

---

17 Wednesday

Moon ☽ in Taurus ♉

---

18 Thursday

Moon ☽ in Taurus ♉

---

19 Friday

Waning Half Moon ☽ in Taurus ♉ 12:36 am
Moon ☽ v/c 7:06 am
Moon ☽ enters Gemini ♊ 8:06 am

The Magic of Hibiscus

Hibiscus is a beautiful, multi-purpose magical flower in the Mallow (*Malvacae*) family. This striking and sensual flower originated in Asia and is magically associated with beauty, love, romance, sensuality, lust, dreams, and divination. Its five petals align it with the geometric shape of the orbital rhythms of the planet Venus, making it a strong flower ally in romantic attraction magic. Combine hibiscus petals, rose petals, patchouli leaf, two tonka beans, a piece of garnet, and a piece of lodestone in a small red velvet bag. Carry it with you to attract romance and passion in your life. You can also make a romantic oil with equal parts rose, vanilla, and ylang-ylang essential oils, blended with carrier oil and hibiscus petals. Wear this blend when you wish to attract romantic partners.

Hibiscus petals can be used for divinatory purposes as well. In the book *Fire Magic,* author Josephine Winter suggests taking a hibiscus flower and assigning it to a person or situation. Take that flower and float it in a bowl of water. Then, observe the way the hibiscus flower acts, moves, and shifts to interpret how the relationship with that person or situation will unfold. If you are looking to do a love reading with tea leaves, try using a blend of hibiscus, rose, dried strawberries, and oolong tea. Look for symbols that indicate love in your tea leaf reading. Hearts are a straightforward indicator of love and romance. Stars can indicate destined love or good luck in love. If you see letters, these can be hints at initials for people who may play a romantic role in your life.

—*Kiki Dombrowski*

20 Saturday

Moon ☽ in Gemini ♊
Mars ♂ in Gemini ♊ 3:56 am

21 Sunday

Moon ☽ in Gemini ♊
Moon ☽ v/c 6:07 pm
Moon ☽ enters Cancer ♋ 8:29 pm

22 Monday

Moon ◑ in Cancer ♋
Sun ☉ enters Virgo ♍ 11:16 pm

Sun enters Virgo (Earth)

23 Tuesday

Moon ◑ in Cancer ♋

24 Wednesday

Moon ◑ in Cancer ♋
Moon ◑ v/c 5:41 am
Moon ◑ enters Leo ♌ 9:10 am
Uranus ♅ ℞ 9:54 am

25 Thursday

Moon ● in Leo ♌
Mercury ☿ enters Libra ♎ 9:02 pm

26 Friday

Moon ● in Leo ♌
Moon ● v/c 2:55 am
Moon ● enters Virgo ♍ 8:25 pm

Spell to Bring Rain

To be used during a drought.

You will need:

- A candle
- A pot of water (and stovetop)
- A wooden spoon or spurtle
- An invocation to your hearth spirit

(optional)
- A small cup of milk, coffee, beer, or wine, or plate of bread and/or butter (optional)

Instructions:

1. Light a candle on the back of the stove. (Optional: Invoke your domestic or hearth spirit and leave an offering of any or all of the above suggestions.) Heat a pot of water to simmer. While you wait for it to steam, sing a song about rain, one you made up or one you've learned, or repeat a prayer or poem about rain. Allow it to bring you into a light trance state, once in which you feel yourself slipping in between the physical and spiritual aspects of existence.

2. When steam rises from the pot (but before the water boils) take your wooden spoon or spurtle and stir the water clockwise. Understand that the steam rising from the pot is an analog of the evaporation process between bodies of water and the sky. Envision the steam rising into the atmosphere, condensing, becoming clouds heavy with moisture. They become darker, thicker, cloaking the sky above you, nearly ready to break into a nourishing storm.

3. Turn off the stove and safely carry the pot of water outside. Pour out the water onto the earth. This is the rain you seek, a microcosmic act of the forces you wish to draw toward you. You are sending a message through this ritual: this is what we need.

4. Go back inside, thank your hearth spirit, and extinguish the candle.

—Heidi Hall

---

27 Saturday

New Moon ● in Virgo ♍ 4:17 am

---

28 Sunday

Moon ◐ in Virgo ♍
Moon ● v/c 11:08 pm

---

29 Monday

Moon ● enters Libra ♎ 5:44 am

30 Tuesday

Moon ● in Libra ♎

31 Wednesday

Moon ◐ in Libra ♎
Moon ◐ v/c 6:44 am
Moon ◐ enters Scorpio ♏ 1:12 pm

1 Thursday

Moon ◐ in Scorpio ♏

2 Friday

Moon ◑ in Scorpio ♏
Moon ◑ v/c 1:22 pm
Moon ◑ enters Sagittarius ♐ 6:40 pm

Using Comfrey to Heal

Comfrey is a traditional and well respected super healer known for its fast action and somewhat incredible healing gifts. *Symphytum officinale,* a native of the British Isles, is a perennial plant that forms big leaves and develops a very deep taproot. It is said that comfrey roots can go up to 10 feet in the ground, so a good rule of thumb is to plant it once and plant it where you want it to grow. Its folk names, knitbone and boneset, speak to its efficacy as a healing herb—it is said that a poultice applied to broken bones would "knit" them back together, healing the break.

A simple way to use comfrey is to create a poultice of the mashed leaves in a piece of cloth or linen and apply to the affected area; hold it there for at least 30 minutes and do this several times to see improvement.

Create a bruise ointment by steeping dried comfrey leaf and/or root in oil, then straining once the oil has taken on the color of the herb. Add some wax to harden up the ointment and use as needed.

Create a liniment by infusing comfrey in rubbing alcohol until the alcohol has absorbed the plant material. It is a good idea to mix it with another agent such as witch hazel extract or vinegar, as alcohol can be drying and may not always absorb into the skin.

Comfrey is also a fantastic fertilizer, so if you want to give your garden a bit of a boost, pour some comfrey tea into the soil of your plants.

—*Stacey Carroll*

3 Saturday

Waxing Half Moon ☽ in Sagittarius ♐ 2:08 pm

4 Sunday

Moon ☽ in Sagittarius ♐
Moon ☽ v/c 9:50 pm
Moon ☽ enters Capricorn ♑ 10:02 pm

September

5 Monday

Moon ☽ in Capricorn ♑
Venus ♀ enters Virgo ♍ 12:04 am

6 Tuesday

Moon ☽ in Capricorn ♑
Moon ☽ v/c 5:43 pm
Moon ☽ enters Aquarius ♒ 11:41 pm

7 Wednesday

Moon ☽ in Aquarius ♒

8 Thursday

Moon ☽ in Aquarius ♒
Moon ☽ v/c 8:33 am

9 Friday

Moon ☽ enters Pisces ♓ 12:43 am
Mercury ☿ ℞ 11:38 pm

Mercury retrograde until October 2

Set in Eastern Daylight Time (EDT)

Nine Herbs Immune-Boosting Tea

The Nine Herbs Charm is an old Anglo-Saxon poem describing the magical properties of nine herbs that were considered sacred to Woden (aka Odin). Of those nine, only nettle is included in the tea below, because the focus here is on promoting healthy immune function and protection from illness. These nine herbs are used in plenty of magical work as well, however. If you'd like to use this tea for multiple magical purposes, simply look up their correspondences and tailor your spell words to your particular goals.

This recipe makes about 1 cup of dried tea blend. If you'd like to make a bigger batch, simply double or triple the amounts of each herb. Use the dried form of each herb for this tea.

You will need:

- 4 tablespoons echinacea
- 3 tablespoons hibiscus
- 3 tablespoons nettle leaf
- 2 tablespoons elderberry
- 2 tablespoons lemongrass
- 4 teaspoons cinnamon bark
- 4 teaspoons lemon balm
- 1 tablespoon licorice root
- 1 tablespoon ginger root

Instructions:

1. Measure and gently combine the herbs into a bowl. Transfer the herb mixture into a jar and label it.
2. Place 1–2 teaspoons in a tea ball or sachet inside your mug. Bring 1 cup of water to a boil, then let cool for 1 minute before pouring over the tea. While you pour, say the following (or similar) words:
   "With these nine magical herbs, the wisdom of the Earth meets the wisdom of the body. I am healthy and whole. Blessed Be."
3. Visualize all the cells in your body growing strong and healthy while you sip.

—Lisa Chamberlain

---

10 Saturday

Full Moon ○ in Pisces ♓ 5:59 am
Moon ○ v/c 8:28 pm

Harvest Moon

---

11 Sunday

Moon ○ enters Aries ♈ 2:47 am

September

12 Monday
Moon ☽ in Aries ♈

13 Tuesday
Moon ☽ in Aries ♈
Moon ☽ v/c 12:52 am
Moon ☽ enters Taurus ♉ 7:40 am

14 Wednesday
Moon ☽ in Taurus ♉

15 Thursday
Moon ☽ in Taurus ♉
Moon ☽ v/c 8:59 am
Moon ☽ enters Gemini ♊ 4:16 pm

16 Friday
Moon ☽ in Gemini ♊

Relaxation Visualization Oil Spell

Unwind and de-stress from a long or difficult day with a quick and easy visualization spell. This spell uses the aromatics of essential oils to facilitate a calm, grounded state of mind. You can also use this combination to help you during ritual or spellcasting.

The carrier oil "carries" the essential oils so they can be safely used on skin. Olive, jojoba, almond, apricot kernel, and rosehip oils make good carriers. If you don't have frankincense, then vetiver, ylang ylang, or clary sage make great substitutes for relaxation. (If you have sensitive skin, do a patch test of any essential oil you haven't used before.) This recipe is adaptable to your scent preferences. Try to repeat this spell often for best results.

You will need:
- 1 tbsp carrier oil of your choice
- 2 drops frankincense essential oil
- 2 drops lavender essential oil
- Small (½ ounce) jar or bottle
- Funnel (optional)

Instructions:
1. Pour the carrier oil into the jar or bottle, using a funnel if needed.
2. Add the essential oils.
3. Seal the container and focus on your intentions for relaxation.
4. Gently roll the jar or bottle in your hands to warm and mix.
5. Chant out loud or silently: *"I am calm, and I am centered."*
6. Now, open the container, take a drop of oil, and anoint your mastoid pressure point, located behind the ears.
7. Visualize a blanket of relaxation settling over your being.
8. Repeat the chant as you breathe in the scents of the oil.
9. Seal and store your oil. Use it to repeat the spell anytime you feel it's needed.   *—Ambrosia Hawthorn*

17 Saturday

Waning Half Moon ☽ in Gemini ♊ 5:52 pm
Moon ☽ v/c 5:52 pm

18 Sunday

Moon ☽ enters Cancer ♋ 4:00 am

Set in Eastern Daylight Time (EDT)

September

19 Monday

Moon ☽ in Cancer ♋

20 Tuesday

Moon ☽ in Cancer ♋
Moon ☽ v/c 11:57 am
Moon ☽ enters Leo ♌ 4:38 pm

21 Wednesday

Moon ☽ in Leo ♌

22 Thursday

Moon ☽ in Leo ♌
Moon ☽ v/c 7:06 am
Sun ☉ enters Libra ♎ 9:03 pm

Mabon / Autumn Equinox 9:04 pm

Sun enters Libra (Air)

23 Friday

Moon ☽ enters Virgo ♍ 3:54 am
Mercury ☿ enters Virgo ♍ 8:04 am

Set in Eastern Daylight Time (EDT)

Mabon Root Spell

Mabon means balance, honoring the shadows, and celebrating the harvest. Our rituals for this Sabbat may involve tapping into our roots (literally and metaphorically) and going deep, asking our ancestors how we can continue to grow and work on ourselves.

For this ritual, peel a large sweet potato and slice off the top so that it's flat. Stab the center of the cut surface and rotate your knife clockwise as your knife pares away bits of potato. This slowly hollows out the center. Continue hollowing until only a ¼ inch of potato remains around the edges. This hollow is where we can begin stuffing the potato with elements that represent our intention: connecting to ancestors. Add rosemary (for spiritual connection, honoring and wisdom) and sweetgrass (to honor and connect). As you place these herbs in, state:

"The witch bottle protects, the cord minds the count, but it's the roots who return home and venture on down. White as bone, like Mother Earth's spine, they wrap and they slinker till they reach the divine. If roots are the bone, then I glide in the marrow, for ancestral wisdom to aid me in peril."

Next, dig a space large enough to bury the potato, top down, along the southern portion of your property. You can also bury the potato in a large container pot and place it in the southern direction. As you dig, bury and replace the soil, say:

"The soil journeys home and so do I. The spiritual conscious has gifts to share, and some have all but fought it. But I take a morsel and save the rest, the wisdom lines my pockets."

—Sarah Justice

24 Saturday

Moon ● in Virgo ♍

25 Sunday ●

Moon ● in Virgo ♍
Moon ● v/c 8:50 am
Moon ● enters Libra ♎ 12:42 pm
New Moon ● 5:55 pm

September/October

26 Monday
Moon ● in Libra ♎

27 Tuesday
Moon ● in Libra ♎
Moon ● v/c 12:20 pm
Moon ● enters Scorpio ♏ 7:15 pm

28 Wednesday
Moon ◑ in Scorpio ♏

29 Thursday
Moon ◑ in Scorpio ♏
Venus ♀ enters Libra ♎ 3:49 am
Moon ◑ v/c 5:20 pm

30 Friday
Moon ◑ enters Sagittarius ♐ 12:03 am

Set in Eastern Daylight Time (EDT)

Theft Protection Folklore Charm

When my mom and I had to clean out my grandmother's house before moving her into assisted living, I came across a number of random objects on windowsills, shelves, under mats, in purses, and in her towels. At first I thought my grandmother just liked collecting things, but when I brought it up with my mom, I learned these were folk charms. I took note of these charms, and took several with me: a horseshoe, a jar of sweet gum seeds known as *witch burs,* and a small collection of "ugly" stones. It's the ugly stones I'll be discussing today.

According to my mother, the "ugly"' stones tell the potential thief you are poor and the items within your home are of no value. As a result, the potential thief leaves your house undisturbed! For added oomph, find stones with a high iron content.

You will need:
- 1–2 "ugly" stones for each window in the home, especially those at ground level or near doors.

Instructions:
Begin by blowing on each stone. This process cleanses the stone and infuses it with some of your energy. When you feel the energy has been cleared from the stone, hold it in your hand, infusing it with protective energy. Whisper instructions to the stone, asking it to keep you and all within your home safe from prying eyes and thieves. Place the stones in your windows. Cleanse and charge them, or "feed" them by giving them an offering of wine or water at least once a month.

Bonus folklore charm: Place a single penny in each of your wallets or purses so you will never run out of money! —*Autumn Willow*

---

1 Saturday

Moon ☽ in Sagittarius ♐
Moon ☽ v/c 5:47 pm

---

2 Sunday

Moon ☽ enters Capricorn ♑ 3:38 am
Mercury ☿ D 5:07 am
Waxing Half Moon ☽ 8:14 pm

Mercury direct

---

3 Monday

Moon ☽ in Capricorn ♑
Moon ☽ v/c 11:48 pm

4 Tuesday

Moon ☽ enters Aquarius ♒ 6:21 am

5 Wednesday

Moon ☽ in Aquarius ♒
Moon ☽ v/c 6:46 pm

6 Thursday

Moon ☽ enters Pisces ♓ 8:46 am

7 Friday

Moon ☽ in Pisces ♓

Witchy Kitchen Sugar Recipe

Sweeten your practice of kitchen witchery by crafting magical sugars with various herbs and spices. These sugars are delicious when sprinkled on fresh fruit or homemade treats like bread and cookies, or stirred into tea or hot cocoa. They can be infused with your intentions for various magical goals.

When choosing ingredients for kitchen witch sugars, look first to your pantry and consult your favorite references for the magical properties of your herbs and spices. To jumpstart you along on the path, try: peppermint for energy, clove for love, cinnamon for protection, ginger for passion, nutmeg for health, or allspice for abundance. Another way to play with the recipe is to try different sugars as your base. You can use whole cane, coconut, turbinado, granulated, caster, or demerara sugars. (Avoid processed white sugar!)

You will need:

- 1–2 tsp dried herb(s)
- 1 cup sugar
- Glass jar
- Food processor (if using whole or hardy herbs) or bowl (if using powdered/ground herbs)

Instructions:

1. Gather your ingredients and cleanse your space.
2. Pour ⅓ cup of sugar into the food processor or bowl. Add 1 teaspoon of herbs, focusing on your intention, and process on the chop setting (or stir) for 10 to 20 seconds.
3. Add another ⅓ cup of sugar and process/stir again.
4. Repeat with the remaining sugar until you have a fine grain herbal sugar.
5. Decant the charmed sugar into your jar and store in a cool, dry place for up to 2–3 months.
6. When ready to use, sprinkle a pinch over your treats, focusing again on your specific intention. —*Severina Sosa*

8 Saturday

Moon ◯ in Pisces ♓
Moon ◯ v/c 7:11 am
Moon ◯ enters Aries ♈ 11:57 am
Pluto ♇ D 5:56 pm

9 Sunday

Full Moon ◯ in Aries ♈ 4:55 pm

Hunter's Moon

10 Monday

Moon ○ in Aries ♈
Moon ○ v/c 10:01 am
Moon ○ enters Taurus ♉ 5:04 pm
Mercury ☿ enters Libra ♎ 7:50 pm

11 Tuesday

Moon ○ in Taurus ♉

12 Wednesday

Moon ◔ in Taurus ♉
Moon ◔ v/c 5:42 pm

13 Thursday

Moon ◔ enters Gemini ♊ 1:08 am

14 Friday

Moon ◔ in Gemini ♊

Ancestor Dinner Ritual

This ritual can be used at Samhain, or any other time of year.

Gather mementos of your ancestors: photos, jewelry, handmade items, etc. and create a small shrine in the center of your table, or nearby. Don't worry if you only have items from your grandparents, or even your parents. Each person is a continuation of the generations before. By connecting with one, you connect with many who came before them. If you have nothing that belonged to your ancestors, you can represent them with a lock of your hair or a small amount of earth and/or water that your ancestors lived on.

Prepare dinner. You might want to make something you associate with your childhood, your family, or your heritage.

Place a candle in the center of your ancestral shrine and light it. You can also light incense if you wish. Place some of your meal on a small plate and set it before the shrine, then sit to eat your portion. Before you eat, say a prayer that honors your ancestors. This is the one I use, but feel free to write your own:

"Beloved ancestors:
Thank you for watching over us, guiding us, and protecting us.
Know that we remember you and love you.
Life is full of challenges, but we do not walk alone.
We hold the wisdom of ages within us, through you.
Instill in us the courage to live honestly and justly.
If there are wrongs, help us right them.
If there are wounds, help us heal them.
Foster us to become better ancestors.
May you ever live in us."

Eat and enjoy your time with your ancestors.   **—Heidi Hall**

---

15   Saturday

Moon ☽ in Gemini ♊
Moon ☽ v/c 12:11 am
Moon ☽ enters Cancer ♋ 12:11 pm

---

16   Sunday

Moon ☽ in Cancer ♋

October

17 Monday

Waning Half Moon ☽ in Cancer ♋ 1:15 pm
Moon ☽ v/c 4:57 pm

18 Tuesday

Moon ☽ enters Leo ♌ 12:45 am

19 Wednesday

Moon ☽ in Leo ♌

20 Thursday

Moon ☽ in Leo ♌
Moon ☽ v/c 6:36 am
Moon ☽ enters Virgo ♍ 12:26 pm

21 Friday

Moon ☽ in Virgo ♍

Set in Eastern Daylight Time (EDT)

The Magical Pothos

Pothos *(Epipremnum aureum)* plants are popular house plants that are both beautiful and easy to maintain. There are many varieties of pothos, including the golden, jade, neon, and marble queen. Even if you don't consider yourself a green thumb, you may find the company of the low maintenance pothos to be magically encouraging.

The pothos was named after the Greek winged god Pothos, the god of passionate longing and unobtainable desire. While that may seem like a challenging aspect, I believe it makes pothos a great ally for those working through feelings of unrequited love. Pothos can assist with the lesson of thriving in places where we are loved and sought after.

Pothos is also known as "devil's ivy," nicknamed for its ability to grow quickly, overtake spaces, grow up trees, and survive with minimal light. Therefore, pothos teaches us that we can survive and persist, even in less-than-perfect scenarios. Pothos is wonderful to have present when you are working to reach your dreams and remain committed to your goals.

Pothos plants are also aligned with prosperity magic and supporting an energy of abundance. Another name for pothos is "money plant," for its bright green colors and leaf shape. Pothos easily propagates roots with simple cuttings, making it an easy plant to share with others.

Finally, pothos is known to clean air, and is therefore wonderful plant for purifying space. In the book *Plant Witchery*, Juliet Diaz observes her pothos swaying when negative energy is in the area. Consider using your pothos to help you to see where to clear and purify energy by placing it in different areas of your house.

—*Kiki Dombrowski*

22 Saturday

Moon ● in Virgo ♍
Moon ● v/c 2:18 pm
Moon ● enters Libra ♎ 9:24 pm

23 Sunday

Moon ● in Libra ♎
Saturn ♄ D 12:07 am
Venus ♀ enters Scorpio ♏ 3:51 am
Sun ☉ enters Scorpio ♏ 6:35 am

Sun enters Scorpio (Water)

24 Monday

Moon ☽ in Libra ♎
Moon ☽ v/c 8:36 pm

25 Tuesday

Moon ● enters Scorpio ♏ 3:19 am
New Moon ● 6:49 am

Solar Eclipse 6:48 am – 2° Sco♏ 00'

26 Wednesday

Moon ● in Scorpio ♏

27 Thursday

Moon ● in Scorpio ♏
Moon ● v/c 12:28 am
Moon ● enters Sagittarius ♐ 6:55 am

28 Friday

Moon ☽ in Sagittarius ♐
Jupiter ♃ enters Pisces ♓ 1:09 am

Herbal Tea for Headaches

There are many different herbs that can help with easing and managing headaches. And unlike most over-the-counter medicines, herbs also have other additional benefits that can help support our systems, aside from just treating the headache. Furthermore, herbal tea often uplifts our spirits as well!

Here are my favorite herbs for managing a headache:

Feverfew (*Tanacetum parthenium*): Used in ancient Greece, feverfew can help with many different conditions, but has made a name for itself as a headache remedy. Although better used for prevention than during a headache, it has been shown to be effective. It is a bitter herb, so make sure you sweeten the tea with honey.

Peppermint *(Mentha spp.):* Peppermint is an all-around powerhouse of an herb. It settles stomachs, helps with gas, eases headaches and more. Plus the lovely minty flavor helps relax and uplift, making it a valuable herb to have in your medicine chest.

White Willow Bark (*Salix alba*): Aspirin is derived from this plant, making it a powerful pain relieving agent. It will help calm the headache, but it is an astringent herb and can be drying.

Valerian (*Valeriana officinalis*): More often used to aid sleep, Valerian helps relax the body and mind, which in turn helps to relieve symptoms of headaches.

Chamomile (*Matricaria chamomilla*): It needs no introduction and is known the world over as a herbal tea of choice. It helps alleviate symptoms of headaches as well as relax the mind and act as a sedative.

As with any treatment, always be mindful of allergies. If you are taking medication or have a history of medical issues, always consult your doctor first.

—*Stacey Carroll*

29 Saturday

Moon ☽ in Sagittarius ♐
Moon ☽ v/c 9:09 am
Moon ☽ enters Capricorn ♑ 9:21 am
Mercury ☿ enters Scorpio ♏ 3:22 pm

30 Sunday

Moon ☽ in Capricorn ♑
Mars ♂ ℞ 9:26 am

31 Monday

Moon ☽ in Capricorn ♑
Moon ☽ v/c 11:14 am
Moon ☽ enters Aquarius ♒ 11:42 am

Samhain

1 Tuesday

Waxing Half Moon ☽ in Aquarius ♒ 1:36 am

2 Wednesday

Moon ☽ in Aquarius ♒
Moon ☽ v/c 6:08 am
Moon ☽ enters Pisces ♓ 1:47 pm

3 Thursday

Moon ☽ in Pisces ♓

4 Friday

Moon ☽ in Pisces ♓
Moon ☽ v/c 5:04 pm
Moon ☽ enters Aries ♈ 6:07 pm

Samhain Spiced Bread for Honoring Ancestors

Celebrate your ancestors with this Autumn-spiced Samhain bread. At your Samhain feast, place a photo or keepsake of your ancestor(s) at your altar, light a candle in front of it, and place a slice of the bread in front of the candle as an offering. Greet and talk to your ancestors while eating your own slice of bread (but leave the offering untouched).

You will need:

- 1½ cups sugar
- 1 cup vegetable oil
- 2 eggs
- 1 cup pumpkin puree
- 1¾ cups flour
- 1 tsp baking soda
- ¼ tsp baking powder
- 1 tsp cinnamon
- ½ tsp nutmeg
- ½ tsp salt
- Loaf baking tin
- Baking rack for cooling

Instructions:

1. Gather your ingredients and clear away unwanted energy from your space.
2. Preheat the oven to 350 degrees Fahrenheit.
3. Combine the wet ingredients (oil, eggs, and pumpkin) in a bowl and mix. Add the eggs one at a time.
4. In another bowl, combine the dry ingredients (sugar, flour, baking soda, baking powder, and spices) and mix.
5. Slowly add the wet ingredients into dry ingredients, adding an additional 2/3 cup water as you stir. Blend until ingredients are fully combined.
6. Pour the batter into a buttered or greased loaf tin and bake for about 45 minutes.
7. Test by placing a cold clean butter knife into the center of the of the loaf. If it comes out clean, the spiced bread is done.
8. Turn finished bread out onto a baking rack to cool.   *—Severina Sosa*

5 Saturday

Moon ○ in Aries ♈

6 Sunday

Moon ○ in Aries ♈
Moon ○ v/c 5:30 pm

November

7 Monday

Moon ○ enters Taurus ♉ 12:15 am

Samhain cross-quarter day 5:36 am

8 Tuesday

Full Moon ○ in Taurus ♉ 6:03 am

Lunar Eclipse 6:01 am – 16° Tau♉ 01'

Frost Moon

9 Wednesday

Moon ○ in Taurus ♉
Moon ○ v/c 7:00 am
Moon ○ enters Gemini ♊ 8:37 am

10 Thursday

Moon ○ in Gemini ♊

11 Friday

Moon ◔ in Gemini ♊
Moon ◔ v/c 5:29 pm
Moon ◔ enters Cancer ♋ 7:23 pm

Inward Solitude Spell

During the transition from Autumn to Winter, spellwork often turns inward. We begin to reflect on our habits of mind and the inner obstacles that limit our growth. But we don't have to wait until this season to turn inward. In any situation of overwhelm, turning inward and calming the mind and body can place us in a healing state, where we're ready to listen to intuitive solutions. Honing these inner skills means we have a built-in space for self-care and meditation, a good asset in anyone's spiritual toolkit.

For this spell, collect dried healing and calming herbs, such as basil, borage, mint, lemon balm, marjoram, juniper berry. Add bits of witch hazel, lavender and pink yarrow. If you like, grind these in a mortar and pestle for a smaller blend. Sprinkle the blend along thresholds of the home. Place the rest in a purple, white or blue sachet and place under your pillow. As you turn in for the night and lay to rest, breathe in deeply, and hold the breath briefly before exhaling. State: *"The cottage hearth is swept of soot, and in its place is warmth. So too is soul, the inner hearth, now strong against the storm."* If your thoughts venture to thoughts that overwhelm or make you uncomfortable, visualize them drifting inward toward the pillow to be absorbed by your herbal sachet. If you wake with these thoughts, repeat the visualization. You can also hold the sachet during meditative practices and visualize the same.

When the sachet has fulfilled its purpose, scatter the herbs outside in the eastern direction, for cleansing, or the southern direction, for banishing.

—Sarah Justice

12 Saturday

Moon ☽ in Cancer ♋

13 Sunday

Moon ☽ in Cancer ♋

November

14 Monday

Moon ☽ in Cancer ♋
Moon ☽ v/c 5:41 am
Moon ☽ enters Leo ♌ 7:48 am

15 Tuesday

Moon ☽ in Leo ♌

16 Wednesday

Venus ♀ enters Sagittarius ♐ 1:08 am
Waning Half Moon ☽ in Leo ♌ 8:27 am
Moon ☽ v/c 6:56 pm
Moon ☽ enters Virgo ♍ 8:04 pm

17 Thursday

Moon ☽ in Virgo ♍
Mercury ☿ enters Sagittarius ♐ 3:41 am

18 Friday

Moon ☽ in Virgo ♍

Set in Eastern Standard Time (EST)

Elemental Magic: Water Blessings

Water is used in many ways in Wiccan ritual and magic—to represent the Water Element, for asperging, for scrying, for crystals elixirs and magical teas, and so on. Consecrating the water we use for ritual purposes is a common practice. But have you thought about blessing the water you drink every day?

Many Witches will recall the Japanese researcher Dr. Masaru Emoto, whose unique experiments measured the effects of words and thoughts on the molecular structure of water. He found that water responds to the energetic vibrations of emotions. Since water makes up around 70% of the human body, it makes sense to treat the water we drink with energetic care.

Try your own water blessing experiment with this quick ritual.

You will need:
- Glass of water
- Bell or chimes

Instructions:
1. Take a sip and make a mental note of how the water tastes and feels in your mouth. Now hold the glass in both hands, close your eyes and take a deep breath or two. Visualize positive energy flowing through your hands and into the water. You might see this as white light, or another color that you associate with joyful and peaceful vibrations.
2. As you hold this vision, say the following (or similar) words:
   "I bless this water with the energies of love, peace, and ease. Blessed Be."
3. Ring the bell over the water. Let the sound vibrations ripple over its surface for a brief moment.
4. Now take another sip. What do you notice is different?

Consider blessing your water every day for a week, and take note of any improvements you notice in your physical and/or emotional well-being.

—Lisa Chamberlain

---

19 Saturday

Moon ☽ in Virgo ♍
Moon ☽ v/c 3:47 am
Moon ☽ enters Libra ♎ 5:58 am

---

20 Sunday

Moon ☽ in Libra ♎

November

21 Monday

Moon ☽ in Libra ♎
Moon ☽ v/c 6:14 am
Moon ☽ enters Scorpio ♏ 12:16 pm

22 Tuesday

Moon ☽ in Scorpio ♏
Sun ☉ enters Sagittarius ♐ 3:20 am

Sun enters Sagittarius (Fire)

23 Wednesday

●

Moon ● in Scorpio ♏
Moon ● v/c 1:15 pm
Moon ● enters Sagittarius ♐ 3:16 pm
New Moon ● 5:58 pm
Jupiter ♃ D 6:02 pm

24 Thursday

Moon ● in Sagittarius ♐

25 Friday

Moon ● in Sagittarius ♐
Moon ● v/c 2:22 pm
Moon ☽ enters Capricorn ♑ 4:19 pm

Set in Eastern Standard Time (EST)

Prosperity Floor Wash

Cleaning one's home is a great way to remove not only dirt and grime, but also negative, stale, and otherwise unwanted energy. However, cleaning can also remove the positive energy, leaving an energetically "blank" canvas in its place. It's important to fill this void with the types of energy we want in our lives, which is where magical floor washes come in! The first time you wash the floor, you should be cleaning for dirt and grime and removing the energies in the space. This is often done by using cleaners such as Pine Sol, ammonia, or vinegar, all of which have strong banishing properties. The second time you wash the floor is when you replace the energy. This floor wash is designed to bring you prosperity, so you may never go without.

You will need:

- 3 cups boiling water
- 1 handful fresh spearmint or 2 tablespoons dried
- 3 drops lemongrass essential oil
- Strainer
- Bucket

Instructions:

1. Bring 3 cups of water to a boil and remove from heat. Place the fresh or dried spearmint in the water and allow to infuse for 5 to 10 minutes. Strain the liquid into a bucket and top with warm water until the bucket is full enough to mop with. Add 3 drops of lemongrass essential oil and stir clockwise while saying, *"Spearmint aplenty, bless me with prosperity. Lemongrass sweet, bring riches and happiness."* Starting at the back of the house and working to the front, wipe down walls and doors, and mop the floors.
2. When done, empty the bucket outside your home to keep the riches close. Flushing this mixture down the drain will flush your money away as well.

—Autumn Willow

26 Saturday

Moon ● in Capricorn ♑

27 Sunday

Moon ● in Capricorn ♑
Moon ● v/c 3:11 pm
Moon ● enters Aquarius ♒ 5:06 pm

28 Monday

Moon ◐ in Aquarius ≈

29 Tuesday

Moon ◐ in Aquarius ≈
Moon ◐ v/c 1:53 am
Moon ◐ enters Pisces ⊬ 7:14 pm

30 Wednesday   ◐

Waxing Half Moon ◐ in Pisces ⊬ 9:37 am

1 Thursday

Moon ◐ in Pisces ⊬
Moon ◐ v/c 9:45 pm
Moon ◐ enters Aries ♈ 11:40 pm

2 Friday

Moon ◐ in Aries ♈

Morning Blues Banishing Spell

A morning meditation is a great way to quiet the mind and banish unwanted thoughts or feelings. Meditation has many physical and spiritual benefits, including reducing stress and increasing your overall well-being. This mini-meditation combines visualization, breathing, and energy work to cast out any stagnant energy before you begin your day.

For the crystal, try a black crystal such as obsidian, jet, or black tourmaline, or a quartz such as clear, rose, or smokey for stronger results. Use a tealight if you'd like to only perform the spell once. If you'd like to repeat this practice often, opt for a larger candle. Yellow is an ideal color choice, for banishing negative feelings and boosting happiness.

You will need:

- 1 candle (tealight or something larger)
- Matches
- Crystal of your choice

Instructions:

1. Gather your ingredients and tools and cleanse your space.
2. Find a comfortable position and light your candle.
3. Hold the crystal in your dominant hand, with both palms facing up.
4. Close your eyes and focus on calming your mind.
5. Breathe slowly in and out.
6. Feel the crystal warm in your hand.
7. Visualize bundling your unwanted thoughts and feelings into a ball in your free hand. Then see that ball of stagnant energy leave your being.
8. Stay in this position. Focus on your breathing until you feel clearer and lighter.
9. To complete the meditation, wiggle your fingers and toes and come back to the moment. When you're ready, extinguish the candle.

—Ambrosia Hawthorn

3 Saturday

Moon ☽ in Aries ♈
Neptune ♆ D 7:15 pm

4 Sunday

Moon ☽ in Aries ♈
Moon ☽ v/c 12:47 am
Moon ☽ enters Taurus ♉ 6:37 am

December

5 Monday

Moon ○ in Taurus ♉

6 Tuesday

Moon ○ in Taurus ♉
Moon ○ v/c 2:02 pm
Moon ○ enters Gemini ♊ 3:49 pm
Mercury ☿ enters Capricorn ♑ 5:08 pm

7 Wednesday   ○

Full Moon ○ in Gemini ♊ 11:09 pm

Long Nights Moon

8 Thursday

Moon ○ in Gemini ♊

9 Friday

Moon ○ in Gemini ♊
Moon ○ v/c 1:14 am
Moon ○ enters Cancer ♋ 2:49 am
Venus ♀ enters Capricorn ♑ 10:54 pm

Set in Eastern Standard Time (EST)

"Money in My Wallet" Magical Dollar Bill Spell

This spell enchants a bill for you to keep in your wallet. It is meant to help keep money in your wallet and attract more money into your life. I've kept a magical dollar bill for financial good luck in my wallet for a few years. While I work hard and maintain a balanced budget, I also like to think that the enchanted bill gives me an extra boost of prosperous magic. It's recommended that you perform this spell on a Sunday. It would be even more beneficial to do this spell during a new moon or when the moon is while in the sign of Taurus.

You will need:

- A dollar bill
- A green candle
- A green or gold ink pen
- Money drawing oil: Consider

using one or a combination of the following essential oils: patchouli, vetivert, cedarwood, and/or bergamot.

Instructions:

1. Anoint the candle with the oil, then light the candle.
2. Take the dollar bill and anoint the corners of the bill with the oil.
3. Draw a symbol three times onto the bill that represent money to you. This could be a dollar sign, the Fehu rune, or a personal sigil for money attraction.
4. Take your pen and write the following around the border on both the front and the back of the bill: *"Money comes to me easily and multiplies endlessly. As I will it, so mote it be!"* If you can, write this in cursive without lifting up your pen.
5. Keep this bill in your purse or wallet.
6. You can also keep a small piece of green jade or aventurine in your wallet alongside this bill.   *—Kiki Dombrowski*

10 Saturday

Moon ☽ in Cancer ♋

11 Sunday

Moon ☽ in Cancer ♋
Moon ☽ v/c 1:49 pm
Moon ☽ enters Leo ♌ 3:09 pm

December

12 Monday

Moon ☽ in Leo ♌

13 Tuesday

Moon ☽ in Leo ♌
Moon ☽ v/c 10:52 am

14 Wednesday

Moon ☽ enters Virgo ♍ 3:46 am

15 Thursday

Moon ☽ in Virgo ♍

16 Friday

Waning Half Moon ☽ in Virgo ♍ 3:56 am
Moon ☽ v/c 2:13 pm
Moon ☽ enters Libra ♎ 2:49 pm

Set in Eastern Standard Time (EST)

Flour Divination Spell

Flour is a Kitchen Witch's go-to. It's rather inexpensive and it serves as the foundation of a vast range of recipes. What's particularly wonderful about flour is that it's historically known as an offering to deities, which is still part of many spiritual practices, and it is held as sacred for its sustenance and abundance. We can also use flour much like we'd use tea leaves or coffee grounds to divine.

You will need:

- Amaranth flour, in a small bowl
- Salt
- Water, in a small bowl, just enough to get the fingertips wet
- Large shallow bowl

Instructions:

1. Grab a hearty handful of flour and rub it between your hands before allowing it to drop back in its small bowl. Do this several times, envisioning your energy flowing to the flour.
2. If you have a particular question, ask it now. Grab a hearty pinch of the flour again from the smaller bowl and, in a clockwise position, drizzle the flour into the large bowl as you move the bowl clockwise, stating, *"Bread-maker's bounty, the seed of the belly. It feeds the heart and the minds of so many. The powder, alight with the plower's enchantment, are made to tell tales when these tones are incanted."*
3. Interpret the symbols made by the drizzled flour by reading clockwise and downward. The symbols nearest the rim and at the top represent the present, and the symbols nearing the bottom and center symbolize the distant future (18 months). Letters, numbers, personal symbols or images, and standard dream symbol meanings can be interpreted. If the reading is positive, meld it with ingredients to bake a bread and manifest the reading. **—Sarah Justice**

---

17 Saturday

Moon ☽ in Libra ♎

---

18 Sunday

Moon ☽ in Libra ♎
Moon ☽ v/c 5:36 pm
Moon ☽ enters Scorpio ♏ 10:31 pm

December

19 Monday

Moon ☽ in Scorpio ♏

20 Tuesday

Moon ☽ in Scorpio ♏
Jupiter ♃ enters Aries ♈ 9:32 am
Moon ☽ v/c 9:45 pm

21 Wednesday

Moon ☽ enters Sagittarius ♐ 2:13 am
Sun ☉ enters Capricorn ♑ 4:48 pm

Yule / Winter Solstice 4:36 pm

Sun enters Capricorn (Earth)

22 Thursday

Moon ☽ in Sagittarius ♐
Moon ☽ v/c 3:15 pm

23 Friday

Moon ☽ enters Capricorn ♑ 2:50 am
New Moon ● 5:17 am

A Yule Feast for the Mothers

In Germanic countries, there are traditions of Wild Hunts led by fierce old Goddesses during the twelve nights of Christmas. These are Goddesses of the wilderness as well as of the hearth, both nature Goddesses and maternal, tutelary Goddesses, or "the Mothers." This feast is a blend of traditions. You can perform it on the Winter Solstice, on Christmas Eve, New Year's Eve, or on "Old Christmas," the night of January 5th.

You will need:

- A meal featuring some kind of grain. Traditional fare is pancakes, or fish and dumplings. I've also done crepes with salmon or shrimp and grits.
- A bowl of hot cereal: porridge, cream of wheat, or grits with a pat of butter
- Optional, if you have children: some candy and small toys as surprise gifts

Instructions:

1. Set the table, light candles, and before you eat, toast to the Mothers whom you hope will visit and bless you. Declare that this feast is held in their honor. Enjoy your meal.
2. Before going to bed, leave the bowl of cereal on your doorstep, your hearth, or beside a window as an offering to the Mothers. If you have children, you can have them leave out their shoes as well and fill them with candies and small toys once they're asleep.
3. Dispose of the offering in the morning. If your children left out their shoes, have fun watching them discover and enjoy the gifts in their shoes. If the Mothers have blessed you, you might find a little extra money in an unexpected place, or a little extra luck may come your way in the new year.

—Heidi Hall

24 Saturday

Moon ● in Capricorn ♑
Moon ● v/c 10:10 pm

25 Sunday

Moon ● enters Aquarius ♒ 2:14 am

December/January

26 Monday

Moon ☽ in Aquarius ≈
Moon ☽ v/c 1:20 pm

27 Tuesday

Moon ☽ enters Pisces ♓ 2:33 am

28 Wednesday

Moon ☽ in Pisces ♓

29 Thursday

Moon ☽ in Pisces ♓
Moon ☽ v/c 1:21 am
Mercury ☿ ℞ 4:32 am
Moon ☽ enters Aries ♈ 5:36 am
Waxing Half Moon ☽ 8:21 pm

Mercury retrograde until January 18

30 Friday

Moon ☽ in Aries ♈
Moon ☽ v/c 12:11 pm

Set in Eastern Standard Time (EST)

Endings and Beginnings: Mercury Retrograde

The final Mercury retrograde of 2022 falls at the tail end of the year, and will stay with us through the first few weeks of 2023. If you're the type to moan and groan at the very thought of Mercury retrograde, here are some useful ways to approach this time:

1. Keep a positive attitude. It can be a sort of relief to have Mercury retrograde to "blame" when things go wrong, but don't start a running tally of all your retrograde mishaps, lest you create more. Remember, the Law of Attraction is always at work!

2. If you haven't already, read Severina Sosa's article "Navigating Retrograding Planets" at the beginning of this planner. There, you'll find tips for gauging what to keep an eye out for during this retrograde, based on your personal astrology.

3. Mercury retrograde is an ideal time to tie up loose ends. So finish up the projects that have been laying around half-done, which will free up your motivation when new inspiration strikes. And if there's a project that you've simply lost the drive for altogether, now is a good time to release it and move on.

4. Sort through old clothes and other "stuff" you're not using anymore and get rid of as much as you can. This clears stagnant energy in your life as well as your closet, and makes room, physically and energetically, for new abundance to come in.

With the right perspective, an end-of-year Mercury retrograde is a great opportunity to celebrate endings and welcome new beginnings. So honor this timely astrological event and approach it with patience and joy.

—Lisa Chamberlain

---

31 Saturday

Moon ☽ in Aries ♈
Moon ☽ v/c 7:44 am
Moon ☽ enters Taurus ♉ 12:09 pm

---

1 Sunday

Moon ☽ in Taurus ♉

2022 at a Glance

JANUARY

M	T	W	T	F	S	S
					1	2
3	4	5	6	7	8	9
10	11	12	13	14	15	16
17	18	19	20	21	22	23
24	25	26	27	28	29	30
31						

FEBRUARY

M	T	W	T	F	S	S
	1	2	3	4	5	6
7	8	9	10	11	12	13
14	15	16	17	18	19	20
21	22	23	24	25	26	27
28						

MARCH

M	T	W	T	F	S	S
	1	2	3	4	5	6
7	8	9	10	11	12	13
14	15	16	17	18	19	20
21	22	23	24	25	26	27
28	29	30	31			

APRIL

M	T	W	T	F	S	S
				1	2	3
4	5	6	7	8	9	10
11	12	13	14	15	16	17
18	19	20	21	22	23	24
25	26	27	28	29	30	

MAY

M	T	W	T	F	S	S
						1
2	3	4	5	6	7	8
9	10	11	12	13	14	15
16	17	18	19	20	21	22
23	24	25	26	27	28	29
30	31					

JUNE

M	T	W	T	F	S	S
		1	2	3	4	5
6	7	8	9	10	11	12
13	14	15	16	17	18	19
20	21	22	23	24	25	26
27	28	29	30			

JULY

M	T	W	T	F	S	S
				1	2	3
4	5	6	7	8	9	10
11	12	13	14	15	16	17
18	19	20	21	22	23	24
25	26	27	28	29	30	31

AUGUST

M	T	W	T	F	S	S
1	2	3	4	5	6	7
8	9	10	11	12	13	14
15	16	17	18	19	20	21
22	23	24	25	26	27	28
29	30	31				

SEPTEMBER

M	T	W	T	F	S	S
			1	2	3	4
5	6	7	8	9	10	11
12	13	14	15	16	17	18
19	20	21	22	23	24	25
26	27	28	29	30		

OCTOBER

M	T	W	T	F	S	S
					1	2
3	4	5	6	7	8	9
10	11	12	13	14	15	16
17	18	19	20	21	22	23
24	25	26	27	28	29	30
31						

NOVEMBER

M	T	W	T	F	S	S
	1	2	3	4	5	6
7	8	9	10	11	12	13
14	15	16	17	18	19	20
21	22	23	24	25	26	27
28	29	30				

DECEMBER

M	T	W	T	F	S	S
			1	2	3	4
5	6	7	8	9	10	11
12	13	14	15	16	17	18
19	20	21	22	23	24	25
26	27	28	29	30	31	

2023 at a Glance

JANUARY

M	T	W	T	F	S	S
						1
2	3	4	5	6	7	8
9	10	11	12	13	14	15
16	17	18	19	20	21	22
23	24	25	26	27	28	29
30	31					

FEBRUARY

M	T	W	T	F	S	S
		1	2	3	4	5
6	7	8	9	10	11	12
13	14	15	16	17	18	19
20	21	22	23	24	25	26
27	28					

MARCH

M	T	W	T	F	S	S
		1	2	3	4	5
6	7	8	9	10	11	12
13	14	15	16	17	18	19
20	21	22	23	24	25	26
27	28	29	30	31		

APRIL

M	T	W	T	F	S	S
					1	2
3	4	5	6	7	8	9
10	11	12	13	14	15	16
17	18	19	20	21	22	23
24	25	26	27	28	29	30

MAY

M	T	W	T	F	S	S
1	2	3	4	5	6	7
8	9	10	11	12	13	14
15	16	17	18	19	20	21
22	23	24	25	26	27	28
29	30	31				

JUNE

M	T	W	T	F	S	S
			1	2	3	4
5	6	7	8	9	10	11
12	13	14	15	16	17	18
19	20	21	22	23	24	25
26	27	28	29	30		

JULY

M	T	W	T	F	S	S
					1	2
3	4	5	6	7	8	9
10	11	12	13	14	15	16
17	18	19	20	21	22	23
24	25	26	27	28	29	30
31						

AUGUST

M	T	W	T	F	S	S
	1	2	3	4	5	6
7	8	9	10	11	12	13
14	15	16	17	18	19	20
21	22	23	24	25	26	27
28	29	30	31			

SEPTEMBER

M	T	W	T	F	S	S
				1	2	3
4	5	6	7	8	9	10
11	12	13	14	15	16	17
18	19	20	21	22	23	24
25	26	27	28	29	30	

OCTOBER

M	T	W	T	F	S	S
						1
2	3	4	5	6	7	8
9	10	11	12	13	14	15
16	17	18	19	20	21	22
23	24	25	26	27	28	29
30	31					

NOVEMBER

M	T	W	T	F	S	S
		1	2	3	4	5
6	7	8	9	10	11	12
13	14	15	16	17	18	19
20	21	22	23	24	25	26
27	28	29	30			

DECEMBER

M	T	W	T	F	S	S
				1	2	3
4	5	6	7	8	9	10
11	12	13	14	15	16	17
18	19	20	21	22	23	24
25	26	27	28	29	30	31

About the Contributors

Lisa Chamberlain is the successful author of more than twenty books on Wicca, divination, and magical living, including *Wicca Book of Spells, Wicca for Beginners, Runes for Beginners,* and *Magic and the Law of Attraction.* As an intuitive empath, she has been exploring Wicca, magic, and other esoteric traditions since her teenage years. Her spiritual journey has included a traditional solitary Wiccan practice as well as more eclectic studies across a wide range of belief systems. Lisa's focus is on positive magic that promotes self-empowerment for the good of the whole. You can find out more about her and her work at her website, **www.wiccaliving.com**

Stacey Carroll is a green path hedge witch, certified herbalist, mad gardener, initiated High Priestess, book lover, and divination enthusiast. Her articles have been published in *Witches and Pagans Magazine, The Crooked Path Journal,* and the now-defunct *Australian Pagan Magazine.* A country girl with a bent sense of humor and a passion for her cats, she has been walking the twisted roads of the witch for many a year now. You can usually find her in the garden, with a book in hand, or in the kitchen baking, loving the life of a country witch and herbalist. Her blog, The Country Witch's Cottage, can be found at **www.thecountrywitchscottage.com**

Kiki Dombrowski is a spiritual researcher and explorer who has spent her life studying mythology, magic, witchcraft, and the supernatural. She lives in Savannah, where she is a professional Tarot card reader, certified life coach, and writer. Kiki has worked with various forms of divination, most notably Tarot, which she began working with over 25 years ago. She has published two books—*Eight Extraordinary Days* and *A Curious Future*—both of which are slated for 2nd editions. She has also been a contributing writer for *Witch Way Magazine.* Kiki received her BA in English and Creative Writing from Southern Connecticut State University. She received her MA in Medieval English from the University of Nottingham. For more information, please visit **www.kikidombrowski.com** or follow her on Twitter at **@KikiD333**

Heidi Hall is a South Central Appalachian folk witch and polytheistic animist. She worships local Gods, as well as some Gods first worshiped in Europe, and attends to the spirits of her ancestors, her household, and others she meets. Her witchcraft includes divination, spirit journeying, and magical work inspired by folk traditions and lore. You can read more from her at **www.thewindseye.com**

Ambrosia Hawthorn is a traveling eclectic witch and card slinger. She is the owner of a witchcraft blog, the Founder of *Witchology Magazine*, and author of *The Spell Book for New Witches, Seasons of Wicca,* and *The Wiccan Book of Shadows*. She found her practice at the age of thirteen and has been studying the craft and her lineage ever since. Ambrosia's goal is to provide material for every kind of witch, using the Wheel of the Year to share new content about all types of magic.

Sarah Justice is the owner of The Tiny Cauldron (www.tinycauldron.com), an online cottage filled with ritual items rooted in authentic traditional witchcraft practices. She is also the co-editor of *Witchology Magazine*, and the Salem Magic teacher at Witch With Me's Academy. She loves anything with candlelight and cobblestones, and enjoys sipping coffee and tending to her wildflower daughter, Winnie.

Severina Sosa is an avid writer about witchcraft and a contributor to *Witchology Magazine*, a publication for modern Pagans. She lives near the Yosemite National Park in California with her husband and an abundance of wildlife. Severina is a practiced herbalist, hedge witch, and astrologer. She works with the elements of the natural world, such as the Earth, the sea, weather, and fire magic. Severina is also a psychic who divines with tools such as the Tarot and the stars.

Autumn Willow is a practicing hedge witch of over 15 years and the author behind the blog *Flying the Hedge*, where she writes about hedge craft, the Wheel of the Year, spirit communication, and folklore. She currently lives in Georgia with her three cats and two chickens, and spends her time teaching high school science, reading, playing World of Warcraft, and remodeling her small home.

Three Free Audiobook Promotion

Don't forget, you can now enjoy three audiobooks completely free of charge when you start a free 30-day trial with Audible.

If you're new to the Craft, *Wicca Starter Kit* contains three of Lisa's most popular books for beginning Wiccans. You can download it for free at:

www.wiccaliving.com/free-wiccan-audiobooks

Or, if you're wanting to expand your magical skills, check out *Spellbook Starter Kit*, with three collections of spellwork featuring the powerful energies of candles, colors, crystals, mineral stones, and magical herbs. Download over 150 spells for free at:

www.wiccaliving.com/free-spell-audiobooks

Members receive free audiobooks every month, as well as exclusive discounts. And, if you don't want to continue with Audible, just remember to cancel your membership. You won't be charged a cent, and you'll get to keep your books!

Happy listening!

More Books By Lisa Chamberlain

*Wicca for Beginners: A Guide to Wiccan Beliefs, Rituals,
Magic, and Witchcraft*

*Wicca Book of Spells: A Book of Shadows for Wiccans, Witches,
and Other Practitioners of Magic*

*Wicca Herbal Magic: A Beginner's Guide to Practicing
Wiccan Herbal Magic, with Simple Herb Spells*

*Wicca Book of Herbal Spells: A Book of Shadows for Wiccans, Witches, and
Other Practitioners of Herbal Magic*

*Wicca Candle Magic: A Beginner's Guide to Practicing
Wiccan Candle Magic, with Simple Candle Spells*

*Wicca Book of Candle Spells: A Book of Shadows for
Wiccans, Witches, and Other Practitioners of Candle Magic*

*Wicca Crystal Magic: A Beginner's Guide to Practicing
Wiccan Crystal Magic, with Simple Crystal Spells*

*Wicca Book of Crystal Spells: A Book of Shadows for Wiccans, Witches, and
Other Practitioners of Crystal Magic*

*Tarot for Beginners: A Guide to Psychic Tarot Reading,
Real Tarot Card Meanings, and Simple Tarot Spreads*

*Runes for Beginners: A Guide to Reading Runes in Divination,
Rune Magic, and the Meaning of the Elder Futhark Runes*

*Wicca Moon Magic: A Wiccan's Guide and Grimoire
for Working Magic with Lunar Energies*

*Wicca Wheel of the Year Magic: A Beginner's Guide to the Sabbats,
with History, Symbolism, Celebration Ideas, and Dedicated Sabbat Spells*

*Wicca Kitchen Witchery: A Beginner's Guide to Magical Cooking,
with Simple Spells and Recipes*

*Wicca Essential Oils Magic: A Beginner's Guide to Working with
Magical Oils, with Simple Recipes and Spells*

*Wicca Elemental Magic: A Guide to the Elements, Witchcraft,
and Magical Spells*

*Wicca Magical Deities: A Guide to the Wiccan God and Goddess,
and Choosing a Deity to Work Magic With*

*Wicca Living a Magical Life: A Guide to Initiation
and Navigating Your Journey in the Craft*

Magic and the Law of Attraction: A Witch's Guide to the Magic of Intention, Raising Your Frequency, and Building Your Reality

Wicca Altar and Tools: A Beginner's Guide to Wiccan Altars, Tools for Spellwork, and Casting the Circle

Wicca Finding Your Path: A Beginner's Guide to Wiccan Traditions, Solitary Practitioners, Eclectic Witches, Covens, and Circles

Wicca Book of Shadows: A Beginner's Guide to Keeping Your Own Book of Shadows and the History of Grimoires

Modern Witchcraft and Magic for Beginners: A Guide to Traditional and Contemporary Paths, with Magical Techniques for the Beginner Witch

Free Gift Reminder

Just a reminder that Lisa is giving away an exclusive, free spell book as a thank-you gift to new readers!

Little Book of Spells contains ten spells that are ideal for newcomers to the practice of magic, but are also suitable for any level of experience.

Read it on read on your laptop, phone, tablet, Kindle or Nook device by visiting:

www.wiccaliving.com/bonus

Did You Enjoy
Wicca Witches' Planner 2022?

Thanks so much for reading this book! I know there are many great books out there about Wicca, so I really appreciate you choosing this one.

If you enjoyed the book, I have a small favor to ask — would you take a couple of minutes to leave a review for this book on Amazon?

Your feedback will help me to make improvements to this book, and to create even better ones in the future. It will also help me develop new ideas for books on other topics that might be of interest to you. Thanks in advance for your help!